Hidden
Threads
of Peru
Q'ero
Textiles

Pages 2–3 Herd of llamas and alpacas. The llamas are larger and have more upcurving tails than the alpacas. Photo by John Cohen, 1957.

Opposite Two women weaving, with a poncho panel on the foreground loom. Photo by John Cohen, 1957.

Right Poncho with *ch'unchu* design in three-color complementary-warp weave. 1.65 x 0.875 m (5 ft 5 in x 2 ft 10½ in), including fringe. The Textile Museum 1974.16.109, gift of Junius B. Bird, Marion Stirling, Mary Frances Recher, and the Peruvian Research Fund.

Overleaf Detail of same.

Hidden Threads of Peru
Q'ero Textiles

**Ann Pollard Rowe
and John Cohen**

MERRELL

in association with

The Textile Museum, Washington, D.C.

First published 2002 by
Merrell Publishers Limited
42 Southwark Street
London SE1 1UN

in association with

The Textile Museum
2320 S Street, N.W.
Washington, D.C. 20008–4088
www.textilemuseum.org

Published on the occasion of the exhibition
Hidden Threads of Peru: Q'ero Textiles
22 March – 4 August, 2002
The Textile Museum, Washington, D.C.

Distributed in the USA by Rizzoli International Publications, Inc.
through St. Martin's Press, 175 Fifth Avenue, New York, NY 10010

A catalog record for this book is available from the
Library of Congress.

British Library Cataloging in Publication Data:
Rowe, Ann Pollard
Hidden threads of Peru : Q'ero textiles
1. Quero textile fabrics 2. Quero Indians – Social life
and customs 3. Quero Indians – Rites and ceremonies
I. Title II. Cohen, John III. Textile Museum
746′ .09853

ISBN 1 85894 148 2 (hardback)
ISBN 1 85894 160 1 (paperback)

Produced by Merrell Publishers Limited
Designed by Brighten the Corners – Studio for Design
Edited by Nicola Freeman

Printed and bound in Italy
Front cover/jacket: Poncho with *ch'unchu* design in three-color
complementary-warp weave (detail, see p. 5)

Contents

Acknowledgments

The Textile Museum is grateful to the following generous donors who have made possible the publication of this volume: Marion Stirling Pugh, The Charles Delmar Foundation, and the Josef and Anni Albers Foundation. In addition, Deborah Bell was helpful in linking us with the Albers Foundation. We also recognize and appreciate the interest of Hugh Merrell in this project. Photographer, filmmaker, and musician John Cohen was seminal in bringing this exhibition and publication into being. For his generous collaboration, as well as his gift of Q'ero textiles, we are deeply grateful. That the process of collaboration has been a pleasure is a great testament to his forbearance. The undertaking has also benefited from the support and enthusiasm of Steven Webster, who shared with us much previously unpublished field data on Q'ero.

At The Textile Museum, we especially thank Ursula E. McCracken, Director, and the Board of Trustees for their support. We are also grateful to other Museum staff members who have contributed directly to the project. Librarian Mary Mallia has secured publications and interlibrary loans. Sonja Nielsen provided the assistance of Brewer Thompson in tracking down and obtaining copies of several additional elusive articles. Lydia Fraser digitized existing photographs of Q'ero textiles in order to make them available in our database. Diego Silva helped with Spanish correspondence. Jennifer Heimbecker coordinated the photography of Textile Museum pieces and ran numerous photographic errands. The photographs of The Textile Museum's Q'ero textiles were taken by Jeffrey Crespi.

For access to the Q'ero collections at the American Museum of Natural History in New York, Vuka Roussakis, Anahid Akasheh, Lisa Whittall, and Laila Williamson were most accommodating. John Cohen photographed the American Museum textiles. I am also indebted to Jeffrey Quilter and Bridget Gazzo for providing access to the superb pre-Columbian library at Dumbarton Oaks. We are also very grateful to Emilio Rodriguez for his generosity with so many of his slides. For the use of the Figueroa and Chambi photographs, we thank Adelma Benavente, Peter Yenne, Edward Ranney, and Teo Allain Chambi. Sonya Cohen Cramer and Leonard Stokes provided valuable assistance with the graphics. We also greatly appreciate the loan of Carol Rasmussen Noble's beautiful shawl and Jordi Blassi's wonderful Carnival photograph. In addition, I am very grateful to Ellen McQueary for translating much of the Müllers' German text.

Finally, I would particularly like to thank Marion Stirling Pugh for her steadfast support for Western Hemisphere acquisitions, research, and publication over many years. For the present project, in addition to the publication funds already mentioned, she contributed to the acquisition funds I used in my fieldwork in the Cuzco area in 1974, and also gave the Museum a magnificent Q'ero poncho she and her first husband had acquired on a visit to a Cuzco-area hacienda in the 1940s (fig. 4.10). This generosity is typical of her interest, which has greatly enriched our collections.

Ann Pollard Rowe
Curator of Western Hemisphere Collections
The Textile Museum

Woman weaving a poncho panel. Photo by John Cohen, 1957.

Right Map of Peru.

Below Map of the Cuzco area.

Opposite Map of the Q'ero and Ocongate areas.

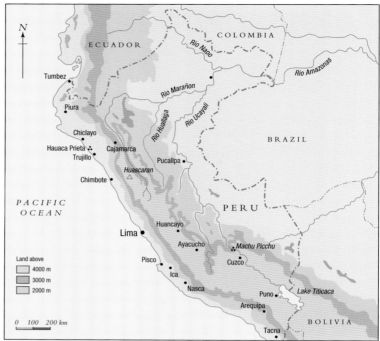

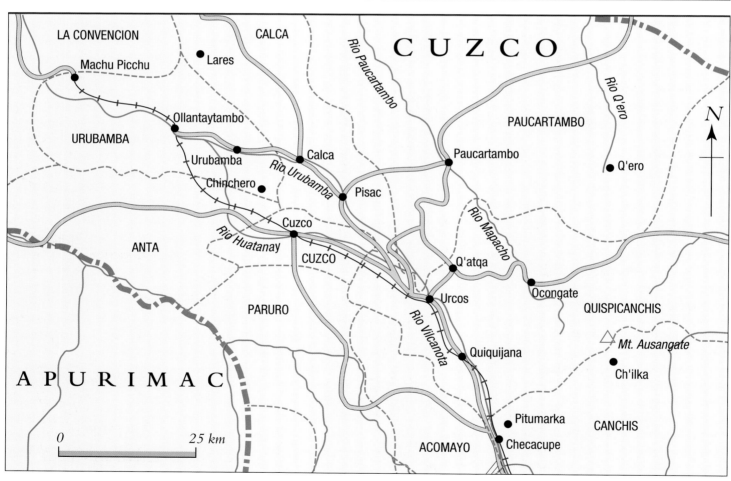

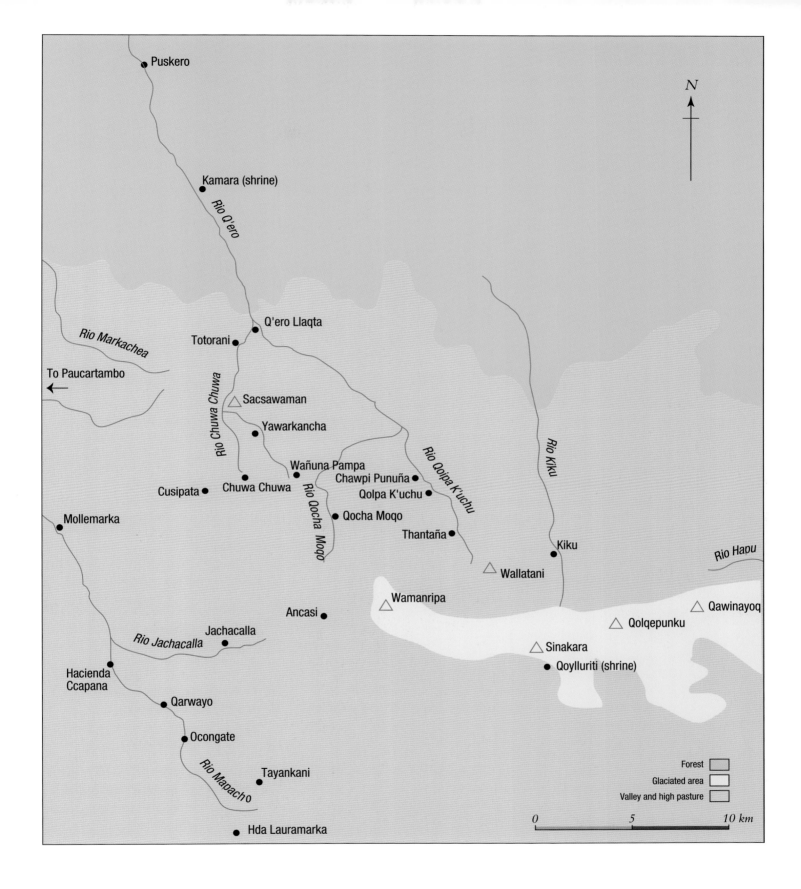

Puskero

Kamara (shrine)

Rio Q'ero

Rio Markachea

Q'ero Llaqta

Totorani

To Paucartambo

△ Sacsawaman

Rio Chuwa Chuwa

Yawarkancha

Wañuna Pampa

Chawpi Punuña

Cusipata   Chuwa Chuwa   Qolpa K'uchu

Rio Qolpa K'uchu

Rio Qocha Moqo

Qocha Moqo

Rio Kiku

Thantaña

Kiku

Rio Hapu

Mollemarka

△ Wallatani

Wamanripa

Ancasi

Jachacalla

Rio Jachacalla

△ Qawinayoq

△ Qolqepunku

△ Sinakara

Hacienda
Ccapana

Qarwayo

Qoylluriti (shrine)

Ocongate

Rio Mapacho

Tayankani

Hda Lauramarka

Forest
Glaciated area
Valley and high pasture

0   5   10 km

Introduction
Why Q'ero?

by Ann Pollard Rowe

The community of Q'ero is more isolated geographically and culturally than most indigenous Andean communities. Because of this circumstance, it offers a view of earlier patterns and practices, some probably nineteenth century or colonial, but others resembling descriptions of Inca life. It is located about 160 km (100 miles) east of Cuzco in southern Peru on the eastern flanks of the Andes mountains. It takes an average of two days on foot or horseback to traverse the 50 km (30 miles) from the nearest vehicular road.

Q'ero is also notable for its exploitation of three different ecological niches at different altitudes, from the alpaca pastures at 3800–4600 m (12,500–15,000 ft) to potato fields at 3100–3700 m (10,000–12,300 ft), to the maize fields at 1800–2100 m (6000–6900 ft).[1] Other Andean communities achieve access to the resources of different ecological zones by trade between separate communities at each level, but Q'ero encompasses them all. This geographic range is the major source of its self-sufficiency and independence, and thus also a significant factor in its degree of cultural preservation.

Outside the community, Q'ero is best known for its textiles and its ritual specialists (paqo). Textiles are the chief artistic expression, made from yarn handspun from the hair of the community's own alpacas and llamas and woven on the indigenous style of staked-out loom. While the pattern-weaving of the whole Cuzco area has certain features in common, that of Q'ero is instantly recognizable within this matrix. Women's shawls and men's festival ponchos and coca bags are decorated with warp-patterned (lengthwise) bands having designs representing principally the ch'unchu, or tropical forest Indian wearing a feather headdress, and inti, the sun, a rayed diamond. As is typical in the Cuzco area, the weavers create these designs by meticulously picking each warp thread in the pattern bands by hand, a time-consuming process that also allows for endless variations and permutations in the patterns. The Textile Museum's collection includes Q'ero women's shawls dating from as early as the late nineteenth century as well as recent examples, illustrating the stylistic development over time. In common with other Cuzco-area weaving, the patterned bands are now considerably wider and the designs bolder than older examples, though less finely spun and woven.

The Q'ero weaving style has other notable features. It makes lavish use of opposing directions of yarn twist in solid-colored areas, a subtlety rare in other Cuzco-area weaving. Q'ero is also one of the few places in southern Peru where men still wear a pre-Hispanic style of tunic and where some wrapping cloths have a horizontal color change in the middle, another pre-Hispanic technique, which together with lengthwise stripes produces a quartered design. While warp-resist dyeing (ikat) is no longer practiced in Q'ero, it does occur in some older ponchos.

Q'ero is also the only place in Peru where a ceremony has been recorded that is conducted specifically in honor of the handwoven textiles produced there, making explicit the value that the community places on this medium of expression (see Chapter 5). This ceremony was recorded by Steven Webster, an anthropologist who did extensive fieldwork there in 1969–70 and again in 1977. Of course his dissertation and published articles contain much useful information about Q'ero, but we are also very pleased that he has been interested in providing us with additional data on this and other customs in Q'ero that are published here for the first time. This new information is credited to him in the text, while previously published information is credited in the notes.

The Textile Museum collection of Q'ero textiles, now amounting to forty-eight examples, had its beginning when I did six weeks of fieldwork researching Cuzco-area textiles in 1974. I did not go to Q'ero, but the style exerted an immediate appeal and I acquired a number of Q'ero textiles for the Museum while in Cuzco. Several were purchased from Oscar Núñez del Prado, the Peruvian anthropologist who had organized and led the first expedition to study Q'ero in 1955, and who was instrumental in helping the community to buy back its land from the local hacienda. Although we subsequently received gifts of individual textiles from several donors, the most significant gift is that from photographer, filmmaker, and musician John Cohen, who has made eight trips to Q'ero over the past forty years (see below). For this book and its accompanying exhibition, we have supplemented our holdings with selections from the extensive collection in the American Museum of Natural History in New York. They have thirty-seven textiles collected by Núñez del Prado (acquired in 1956), and fifty-one textiles plus six additional dance accessories (chiefly featherwork) collected by John Cohen (acquired in 1957). In addition, we have used a few pieces from private collections.

A considerable amount of information about Q'ero can be found in the anthropological literature on account of the interest in the community's conservatism, but this information is not easily accessible. Much of it has been published only in Spanish, and even the English sources are not necessarily easy to find. It therefore seems well worth including a summary here. Our further aim is to provide a general description of the relevant features of Cuzco-area weaving in its social context, as it is practiced in Q'ero in particular. Information on Q'ero textiles has been gathered from the fieldwork of Núñez del Prado, Cohen, and Webster, some of it previously unpublished, as well as from the published literature and the textiles themselves. I have listed all the works of Gail Silverman-Proust (now Silverman) on Q'ero textiles that I consulted (a few additional ones are referenced in her 1998 book). While I have cited such factual information as she provides, I do not find her theories convincing. Our book takes a different approach to the subject.

Both John Cohen and I have contributed text to this book, and we have each edited the other's work. Because the subjects we each were writing about overlapped, it has been difficult to assign individual authorship to specific sections, apart from these introductions. In general, Cohen's text is based more on direct field experiences and includes anecdotes. So, for example, the description of the llama and alpaca festivals in Chapter 5 is by him, as is the section on aesthetics in Chapter 4, and the opening and closing paragraphs of Chapter 1. I have written the text that is compiled from published and other unpublished sources, and which is based on analysis of the textiles. Thus, I wrote most of Chapters 2 and 3, on the textile repertoire. We are also grateful to Steven Webster for reading and making suggestions on an advanced version of the entire text.

We use the title *Hidden Threads* partly because of the remoteness and isolation of this community. But another reason has to do with the structure of the weaving itself, in which some threads are hidden inside the fabric, so that one face has a red and white design while the other is black and white (see Chapter 3). While this structure is also used in some other Cuzco-area communities, it is carried to virtuosic heights in Q'ero. These textiles are testimony to the achievement of the Q'ero weavers, their skill, persistence, sense of beauty and invention, which reflects our own sense of art.

Notes

1. These elevations (and the distance from Cuzco) are from Webster 1972a. Slightly different ones are given in Webster 1972b, which was written before the fieldwork was complete.

Introduction Working in Q'ero

by John Cohen

I went to Peru initially to research a master's thesis about the contemporary weaving of the Peruvian Indians as part of my degree program in Fine Arts (painting) at Yale University in 1956–57.[1] The topic was my own. Since I was an art student and not a weaver, I had decided to learn the weaving processes in Andean rather than European terminology. The purpose of my visits to the various regions was to gather information about how the work was done, the names of the loom parts in the Quechua and Aymara languages, descriptions of patterns, and the weaving processes involved.

I had been motivated by my own aesthetic dialogue with pre-Hispanic weavers of Paracas textiles about decisions they had made two thousand years earlier. I was taken with the beauty of these large embroidered fabrics that had been unearthed in the 1920s by Peruvian archaeologists.[2] There were some on display at The Brooklyn Museum and I was absorbed by their complexity, visual richness, and technical excellence. The repeated sequences of colors and

the deliberate interruptions to these sequences raised questions that could not be answered in the books of that time. That is why I decided to go to Peru, to study with the descendants of that tradition, and to talk to the people who did the weaving.

Before the trip I spoke with Junius Bird, Curator of South American Archaeology at the American Museum of Natural History in New York and an expert on Peruvian textiles. He gave me a questionnaire about weaving that he had written to guide my work as well as supplying funds to collect textiles and looms for the American Museum.[3] He specifically requested information on warp-resist dyeing (*ikat*) and on the use of *khipus* (counting devices). I also had letters of introduction from Josef and Anni Albers. (I was studying with Joseph Albers at Yale.) The introductions were to Francisca Mayer, a former weaving student of Anni Albers from Black Mountain College, who had a weaving studio in Huancayo for many years, and to Jorge Muelle, the director of the

Archaeological Museum in Lima. Muelle laid out for me a map of places where indigenous hand-weaving practices remained strong in Peru. The name of Q'ero was not on that map.

At that time Q'ero fabrics were not featured in the Cuzco stores that sold weaving to tourists. I only heard of Q'ero by accident. The Cuzco archaeologist Manuel Chavez Ballón told me of a place where they "weave from the left." This intriguing idea did not make sense to me, since I knew weaving was a process that uses both left and right to pass the weft through the warp. Since the uses of the left and right hands were issues mentioned on Bird's weaving questionnaire, however, I was curious to check out this information. So when the opportunity came to travel to Q'ero, I took advantage of it.

On my first journey into Q'ero in November 1956, I traveled with Eduardo De Bary, the son of a wealthy man who owned the Ccapana hacienda adjacent to the region of Q'ero. People in Q'ero were obsequious towards us, speaking

16

in unnaturally high, tense voices that communicated a message of powerlessness, as if to say, "Don't hit me." In the days of the hacienda, they had been constantly mistreated. We were viewed as representatives of power and in this atmosphere it was difficult to get close to any weavers. I had already viewed some beautiful Q'ero fabrics on display in the home of Sr. De Bary, for he recognized their excellence, and the Q'eros would sell their work to him.

In Q'ero I saw some finely woven, distinctive fabrics being worn, and was able to purchase several excellent shawls (*llikllas*). Only a few women were actively weaving at that time, however. The damp, foggy weather made it difficult to work outside. At an altitude of around 4300 m (14,000 ft) we came upon isolated clusters of stone huts, and encountered only a few women and infants there. They told us that everyone else was away: the children in the high pastures with the flocks of alpacas and llamas; the men further down the mountain working in the potato fields.

This first visit to Q'ero was a rushed expedition. De Bary was there to explore and hunt and he did not share my interest in weaving production. During this trip I was nevertheless able to obtain much of the basic information about the names of the Q'ero loom parts and the different designs on the fabrics. I traded my harmonica for a beautiful knitted hat (*ch'ullu*). I inquired so persistently about Q'ero weaving that they told me that newly made textiles would be worn at their Carnival celebration, which was very different from that of other communities around there. Based on this information I was determined to return for that event in February 1957, and although we planned to go together, De Bary decided to stay in Cuzco for the Carnival ball given by the wealthy landowners of Cuzco.

I made this second trip accompanied by a good-humored majordomo from the Ccapana hacienda, Isidro Aragon, who entertained the Q'ero with his talk. We sat on the ground with them and shared food, and relationships were

warmer. Although I arrived too late for Carnival, I was able to gather a great deal of information about the making of the fabrics, and to purchase whatever the people were willing to sell. I obtained some extremely fine and ancient Q'ero textiles with designs that were no longer being produced, though I was unaware of their antiquity or scarceness at that time. No one would part with their looms, however, since they were too precious and personalized a tool. Moreover, the wood had to be brought from the distant jungle.

Part of my collection was presented to the American Museum in 1957, while I kept a representative sampling for myself to study and show to hand weavers. Over the years, as I made subsequent trips to Q'ero, I obtained more textiles, basing my purchases on stylistic and structural ideas that had been generated by earlier ones. In 1999 I donated my collection to The Textile Museum, which has provided the basis of the present book and exhibition.

I returned to Q'ero many times in the following forty years, both to record the music of the Q'ero people and to produce, direct, film, and edit four documentary films. On the trip in 1964, accompanied by my wife and a mestizo guide, we were made to feel welcome. In some homes, people sang for us freely and we recorded their music. Recordings made on this trip were included on a set of LPs issued by the Smithsonian Folkways label in 1966 as *Mountain Music of Peru*, and reissued on CD in 1991. I made a film of the same title in 1983–84.

In 1976–77 I went again, in order to make two films about the community, *Qeros: The Shape of Survival* and *Peruvian Weaving: A Continuous Warp for 5000 Years*. The weaving film includes an interview with Junius Bird and footage of his excavations at the pre-ceramic site (*c.* 3000 BC) of Huaca Prieta on the north coast. My guide on this trip was a former majordomo who had also worked for miners in Q'ero and was *compadre* to a few families. The relationship became complicated. He addressed the Q'eros as an authority figure, and they responded as powerless. But my film assistant Emilio Rodriguez and myself sat with the Q'eros,

shared our food, sleeping bags, and so on with them and got on much better (see photo p. 17). In this climate, the Q'eros became firm and assertive, and even jokey. Women would contradict us, tell us off to our faces, and sometimes be open with us. This was partly due to the *compadre* relationship since we also became *compadres* to various Q'ero families.

By 1983, although the *compadre* relationships remained close, outside influences and political propaganda created an atmosphere of hostility in some people. In 1984 I made a failed attempt to film the Carnival celebration. As far as I knew, it had never been seen by outsiders, and the community was very apprehensive about it. The situation was further complicated by the presence of a Japanese film crew that was there at the same time. Although neither of us was allowed to film the event, and my crew was severely beaten and stoned by some intoxicated Q'eros, I was able to get a sense of what part the music and textiles played in the celebrations.[4] In 1989 I returned to Q'ero with Peruvian anthropologist Juan

Núñez del Prado (son of Oscar), and we successfully documented the Carnival rituals on film (*Carnival in Q'eros*, 1990). Núñez del Prado was friendly with the Q'eros and everything went smoothly.

As a visitor to Q'ero over many years, I have found that engaging in this extended dialogue with the Q'ero view of the world has changed my own. It has offered an alternative way of looking at almost everything: survival, continuity, individual creativity, art, nature, and ways to approach the spirit. An examination of their textiles is one way into the richness of Q'ero thought.

One particularly fine weaver I worked with over the years was Nicolasa Quispe Chura, from the hamlet of Wañuna Pampa. I first met her in 1956 when she was about twelve years old (see photo p. 20). Twenty years later I met her again while making my first film there (fig. 3.3), and took notice of the excellence of some of the weaving she wore. It was she who knew how to weave the carrying cloth with the four-color field (figs. 2.19, 3.27), and she also eventually allowed me to

Nicolasa Quispe Chura
(right), with her sister
Andrea and little brother
Raymundo, standing
before the mountain
that dominates their
hamlet of Wañuna
Pampa. Photo by
John Cohen, 1956.

purchase the extremely fine shawl she was wearing during the filming (figs. 3.7, 4.15). From her I came to realize the hardships of life in Q'ero. She looked directly into my camera and told her story:

My baby son, as well as my husband, got sick while we were far from home. I brought the baby back, and my daughter followed me like a little puppy, weak and breathless. As we got here my husband got completely ill, and he decided to go to his father's house. He said, "Because if I am going to be sick, it might as well be at my father's house. Here, who is going to take care of me?" I stayed behind, and since I was sick and my baby was sick, the baby died. It was a night and a day before he was buried. Meanwhile I sent word to my husband but he did not respond even with a bit of clothing for the dead baby. So I had to take cloth from my own burial gown, to make a gown in which to bury the baby, so I buried him myself.[5]

Confronted with her tragedy, I tried to help her in any way possible. And I was struck by the responsibility that accompanies fieldwork. Weavers are not just informants, but have complex human lives like anyone else. In commiseration and appreciation, I gave Nicolasa an excellent red axe with the instruction to save it for her daughter's dowry. Having such a wonderful axe might get her a wealthier husband, and hopefully give her an easier life.

In 1983 I returned and asked after Nicolasa. She and her husband were no longer together and she was now living in Totorani. I noticed that the red axe was in her brother's house, used but in good condition. In 1989 I learned that she had died. Yet the hardships of her life did not prevent her from doing wonderful weaving, and her carrying cloth and shawl are presented here to illustrate the richness of the tradition that she represents.

Notes

1. Cohen MS.
2. See, for example, Paul 1992.
3. Bird 1960.
4. Cohen 1987.
5. Cohen 1979.

Chapter One Life in Q'ero

There is a distinctive visual order to the Q'ero landscape and its transition into the lives of its inhabitants. Jagged mountain peaks engage with the sky in all directions (figs. 1.1, 1.2), and the clouds from the jungle rise from below, abruptly obscuring the sun, and sometimes enveloping the whole visual field in a deep fog. The prevalent color scheme in the high pastures consists of gray rocks, often showing reddish mineral stains, with yellowed and tan grasses. Brighter fields of green grass are seen around the houses. This grass is cropped close by the herds of alpacas, llamas, and sheep, which return from the pastures every night to sleep in the corrals beside the stone-and-thatch huts.

No trees or bushes grow at this altitude, where people spend most of their time. There are small streams everywhere, fed by the melting snows from the high mountain glaciers, and small channels are dug into the ground that lead the water to wherever it is needed (fig. 1.2). There are corbelled bridges of uncut stones crossing

Fig. 1.2 Q'ero
landscape, including
some houses and
alpacas. Note also the
water-drainage ditch.
The woman is using
her topmost skirt for
carrying. Photo by John
Cohen, 1957.

the larger streams, and deep channeled
paths in the earth formed by the daily
passage of hundreds of llamas and alpacas
as they go up to and return from the high
pastures. The entire terrain is defined by
an endless criss-crossing of subtly inclined
paths made by the animals (fig. 1.1).

From a distance, the clothing of the
Q'eros appears appropriately drab and
functional, with gray ponchos and black
tunics and pants worn by the men, and
dark skirts and flat-rimmed hats worn
by the women. But as with a flower, the
closer you get, the richer it appears
(fig. 1.4). Up close, you experience the
vibrant reds and pinks of the women's
blouses, and the brightly colored stripes
and edges on the men's garments. The
women's shawls display fabulously intense
bands of red and white patterns set off
against black stripes, and in their hats they
often wear bright-red flowers picked from
the mountainside. The yarns used to join
textile parts together are often an array
of vivid colors, along with equally bright
tassels and fringes. It is as if the people
are the flowers in this vast landscape.

Beyond its use to identify the region
and its inhabitants, the word *q'ero* (or
qero, *qeru*, *kero*, and other variants) refers
to a wooden drinking cup in the Inca
language, and Inca and colonial examples
are well known. The cups most commonly
used in Q'ero in recent years are made
in Paucartambo and have a footed shape,
probably due to Spanish influence, but
the cup illustrated here, collected in
Q'ero by John Cohen in 1957, has an
Inca shape (fig. 1.3). The cups were and
are used for ceremonial drinking of maize

beer during festivals (see Chapter 5).

The name of the place has been spelled in various ways – Qqueros, Q'eros, Qeros, Q'ero – with the last spelling most common among anthropologists who have worked there. The letter "q" indicates a clicking sound pronounced in the back of the throat, for which there is no English or Romance language equivalent. The apostrophe indicates a glottal stop, which is made by closing the space around the vocal cords, causing a kind of hesitation (as for example between the "n" and "e"

in "inevitable"). Although the word for the cup is usually pronounced and spelled without a glottal stop, anthropologist Steven Webster says that the people of Q'ero confirm that in their minds it is the same word. He also notes that the Q'eros often exaggerate their glottal stops with gusto, and this may explain the spelling of the place name. The final vowel may be pronounced as either "o" or "u" or somewhere in between. The sound is written "o" in hispanicized transliterations, but usually with "u" in orthographic

systems. We have not ventured to change the most common spelling here, which otherwise might be transliterated Qeru.

The Inca language is usually called *runa simi* (the people's language), or sometimes *Inka simi* by those who speak it, but Quechua by others. It is still spoken by many indigenous people in highland Peru, including the people of Q'ero. Inhabitants of more remote areas, like Q'ero, may speak little or no Spanish. In Q'ero, this name refers to the place. Indigenous people call themselves *runa* (people), and

Fig. 1.4 People working in a potato field, with the Q'ero valley in the background. Photo by Emilio Rodriguez, 1976–77.

Fig. 1.5 Man with a cow decorated for a fertility ceremony, Mollemarka. The poncho is in the style of the Ocongate area with supplementary-warp patterning, worn inside-out. Photo by John Cohen, 1957.

in doing so they distinguish themselves from more hispanicized Peruvians, the cholos, mestizos, and creoles. In English, however, it is convenient to refer to the people of Q'ero as Q'eros.

Q'ero in the larger sense refers to a cultural zone consisting of several politically and historically distinct communities, each in separate but adjacent valley systems radiating north, east, and southeast downward from the glaciers of the Ayakachi mountain complex to the tropical forest below (fig. 1.4). These communities

share certain cultural features including a common textile style, but are each organized differently in response to environmental factors. The most central is that organized around the ritual center of Q'ero Llaqta (Q'ero Place), sometimes referred to by outsiders as Hatun Q'ero (Big Q'ero). This village, although containing the largest number and size of houses in the area, is virtually deserted for most of the year. It is inhabited only during the major community festivals, when there is work to be done in the area, or en route to or from the maize fields. It was, however, probably historically important as a church and administrative center for the hacienda and in the post-hacienda era has become a center for schooling. The main residences are in eight smaller hamlets of four to twelve families as well as several isolated farmsteads, located near the pasturelands, which include a total of around 400 people. Most of the anthropological work has been done in the hamlets associated with Q'ero Llaqta since it is the most isolated and conservative community as well as being best situated to take advantage of the three different ecological zones.[1]

Among the other communities of the Q'ero cultural area, Kiku, to the east of Q'ero, has a relatively flat area near the pasturelands, so there is a single village here that functions both as main living quarters and ritual center. Kiku has relatively little pasture suitable for alpacas, however. Hapu, to the east of Kiku, has a dispersed settlement and an empty ritual center like Q'ero Llaqta, but must share Kiku's maize-producing zone. Its high pastures are also very limited. This situation has led to people having to work

Fig. 1.6 Ch'ilka woman's shawl. The patterned stripes are in complementary-warp weave. 64.5 x 52 cm (25½ x 20½ in). The Textile Museum 1974.16.2, gift of Junius B. Bird, Marion Stirling, Mary Frances Recher, and the Peruvian Research Fund.

Ocongate area in 1957 in Mollemarka (fig. 1.5). It is possible, however, that communities of higher elevation in that area are more closely affiliated culturally with Q'ero or that the textile style was formerly more like Q'ero.

The indigenous people living in the area around and between the market towns of Ocongate and Paucartambo (the provincial capital), on the western slopes of the Andes south of the Q'ero area, do not appear to have an ethnic group identity, but the textile style is distinct from Q'ero, as noted. Some distance southeast of the Q'ero cultural area is another zone of glaciated mountains including the impressive Mt. Ausangate, and on the other side of this is another cultural area, centering on the village of Ch'ilka. Despite the mountain barriers, people from Ch'ilka come to Q'ero at the time of the maize harvest to exchange alpaca and llama meat and fiber for maize (fig. 1.6). The village of Pitumarka, at a lower elevation to the west of Ch'ilka, has a close relationship with Ch'ilka but a distinct textile style is also present (figs. 1.7, 1.8).[3]

The main residences of the people affiliated with Q'ero Llaqta (hereafter referred to as Q'ero) are in small hamlets at 4100 m (13,500 ft) near the alpaca pastures, since the animals need to be tended year round. A family generally has both a living house and a storehouse for freeze-dried potatoes, maize, fuel, and so on. Items are stored in bags, or in cylindrical containers made of bamboo slats. The men tending the agricultural fields live in huts near either the potato fields or the maize fields during the times of year when those need most attention.

outside the community and to the demise of its major rituals. Totorani, to the west of Q'ero, shared the maize zone of Q'ero before ceasing to grow maize altogether. It has dispersed hamlets and a ritual center near the potato fields. Less information is available about other communities reported to belong to the Q'ero cultural zone to the west of Totorani, including K'achupata, Markachea, and Mollemarka, but they tend to be more acculturated.[2] John Cohen photographed a man wearing a poncho of the neighboring style of the

Fig. 1.7 Pitumarka woman's shawl, probably woven c. 1900. The patterned stripes are in complementary-warp weave. 96 x 87 cm (37¾ x 34¼ in). The Textile Museum 1983.7.3, Latin American Research Fund.

The houses in the herding hamlets comprise a single room and have no furniture. There are no windows, and the door is in the wide side, usually facing the sunrise. All activities take place on the ground. There is a cooking area with a clay stove structure that holds the metal cooking pots and clay pots (both purchased). Gourds are also used as containers. A wooden rack against one wall stores fuel, consisting of dried dung and cactus parts. A length of bamboo is used to blow air on the glowing embers. There is no chimney or smoke hole, so the smoke simply filters through the thatch roof. An assortment of hooks and platforms are suspended from the rafters, often with a piece of meat hanging in the smoke. Utensils, bowls, and such are stored on shelves extending out from the interior stone walls, and other objects including textiles are housed in niches between the stones or under the eaves of the roof. A stone platform with a semicircular rocking stone is used to grind grain and freeze-dried potatoes. The floor is flat dirt, and people sit and sleep on

Fig. 1.8 Pitumarka woman's shawl, probably woven *c.* 1960. The main patterned stripes have a *ch'unchu* design (see Chapter 4). The patterned stripes are in complementary-warp weave and with supplementary warp. 77.5 x 88.5 cm (30½ x 34⅞ in). The Textile Museum 1974.16.39, gift of Junius B. Bird, Marion Stirling, Mary Frances Recher, and the Peruvian Research Fund.

woven blankets or animal fleeces. The only light is from the low doorway. The door itself and its framework are of wood from the jungle, cut and shaped many years before, and moved to a new house when the old one is abandoned. The doors have a large wooden lock and key contraption, a Spanish colonial introduction. At night a few candles are lit, but when John Cohen first arrived in Q'ero in 1956, most homes had only a small lamp consisting of a wick made from dried plant leaves set in a container holding melted animal fat.

In contrast to most other indigenous Andean houses, there are no guinea pigs (an Andean domesticate) scurrying around the interior. Cats are rare but John Cohen saw one that was passed from house to house to catch the occasional mouse. Hungry, unfriendly dogs stay outside the door, dependent on scraps such as potato peels for their food. Their job is to keep predators from the flocks at night. If a puma or fox is thought to be lurking nearby, a young person is sent out to sleep in a small straw hut alongside the corral.

Fig. 1.9 Herd of alpacas, showing some of the different colors. Photo by Emilio Rodriguez, 1976–77.

Herding

Herd animals are kept at altitudes above the agricultural zone, that is, above 3800 m (12,500 ft), which is also where the best pastures are found (fig. 1.9). In Q'ero, alpacas and llamas are of the greatest importance. The herd size ranges from ten to more than a hundred animals, with llamas comprising about 25% of each family's herd. These relatives of the camel were domesticated in the highlands of southern Peru and northern Bolivia some 4000 years ago. Alpacas are considered the primary form of wealth in Q'ero.[4] They are most valued for their fine hair, which is made into clothing and other textiles. A small surplus of alpaca hair is traded for goods from outside the community. Llama hair is also spun and woven, but usually into more heavy-duty utilitarian textiles, such as blankets, carrying cloths, transport sacks, and ropes.

Alpacas are more susceptible to disease and thrive on a smaller variety of plants than llamas. They require pasturing in wet grasslands, called *waylla* in Q'ero, between

Fig. 1.10 Llama train crossing a bridge, carrying maize up from the jungle. Photo by Emilio Rodriguez, 1976–77.

4000 and 4600 m (13,000 and 15,000 ft), which are watered by glacial run-off. Alpacas especially favor dwarf reeds in tussock formations (cushion plants). The number of alpacas in the community is conditioned by the amount of available pasture of the appropriate kind. Alpacas are also less responsive to human direction than llamas and require more attention in herding. The cold temperatures at high altitudes protect the animals from parasites and are thought to promote higher quality fleece. A small proportion of the alpacas has longer and straighter hair than usual and these animals are called *suri*. Alpacas and llamas have a wide range of natural colors of hair (fig. 1.9) and there is a large vocabulary for describing the different colors and color patterns on the animals.[5]

Male llamas are used to transport the harvest of maize and potatoes to the houses where it will be stored, as well as dung from the pastures to the potato fields, where it is used as fertilizer (fig. 1.10). They can carry loads of about 25–30 kg (55–65 lbs). A llama train has two or three leaders, which are decorated with extra tassels and bells (fig. 1.11). They set the pace and provide an example in the more dangerous places on the route to the jungle, such as on fragile log bridges and along deep ravines. Llamas

**Fig. 1.11 Lead llama
with tassels and bells.
Photo by Emilio
Rodriguez, 1976–77.**

can traverse these steep and perilous paths more easily than European animals and with less damage to the landscape.

Llamas and alpacas are fastidious and defecate in specific places, which makes it easier to gather the dung to use for both fertilizer and fuel. People sweep it up with their hands and then place it in conical piles, to await future use. The base of a cactus plant is also sometimes used for fuel. The meat of both llamas and alpacas is eaten, mostly of animals who have died of natural causes. Animals are slaughtered only for feasts and rituals, by inserting a blade behind the occipital bone to sever the spinal column. Blood, viscera, and heads are cooked in stews, and some cuts of meat may be roasted. Commonly, the extra meat is dried and smoked for later use in soups. The sinew is also used as cordage, for example in roof construction (fig. 1.13) and bindings on tools.

Most families also have a few sheep. Sheep have a higher reproduction rate than camelids and have less specific pasture requirements than alpacas, but the wool is of considerably less value. They also have a far lower intelligence than llamas and alpacas and are more vulnerable to predators, so it is much more work to keep them. According to Steven Webster, the wool is mostly sold to traders rather than locally woven. By 1979–80, however, more sheep's wool was being locally used, since alpaca hair brings a higher price on the market.[6] Families may also have a horse or two, for trading expeditions as well as for status and ceremonies. Relatively few people have cows or pigs.

Fig. 1.13 Roofing a
house. Photo by
John Cohen, 1957.

Fig. 1.12 Raymundo
Quispe Chura and
llama friend, Wañuna
Pampa. Photo by
John Cohen, 1977.

The herding is done mostly by older children and young adults. Herders drive the animals from the hamlet to the pasture in the morning and back again at dusk. They need to protect the herd from predators such as pumas, foxes, and condors and to control straying, which they do by means of shouts and slingshots. When a herder spots a condor, he or she calls out to other nearby herders to alert them. The herder often spins, or sings (girls) or plays the flute (boys) to pass the time. Herders of neighboring flocks may also

converse. The animals belong to individuals. Children are given animals at a young age so that they will feel more responsibility for them and so that they will have a herd of viable size when they become adult.

In Q'ero, people consider the animals to be part of their family (fig. 1.12). Each animal has a name and the herders are aware of the needs and condition of every animal in the flock. One song to the animals says:

Because you eat, we eat
Because you drink, we drink
Because you are, we are.

Fig. 1.14 Potato fields, including the fallow fields used in other years. Photo by John Cohen, 1976.

Tuber cultivation

The principal crop is potatoes, an Andean domesticate, which constitutes 80% of the diet. Several dozen different varieties are cultivated, of various shapes, sizes, and colors, each with its own name. Some are bitter potatoes, which will grow at a higher altitude than regular potatoes, up to 4200 m (13,750 ft). Below 3100 m (10,000 ft) arable soil is scarce in the Q'ero territory. The bitter potatoes are either leached in running water and then freeze dried (*moraya*) or leached and

exposed to alternate frost and sun to desiccate and ferment the pulp, a process hastened by tromping on them with the bare feet (to make *chuñu*). The potatoes can be stored for long periods in this form. Several varieties of other native tubers such as *oca*, *ullucu*, and *añu* are also grown. The Q'eros know at exactly what altitude each variety will grow best. Some families cultivate small fields of *tarwi* (a legume), *kañiwa* (a seed crop), amaranth, or *kulis* (an herb) within walled areas in order to keep the cold breeze off the plants. The

Fig. 1.16 Hut in the
maize fields. Photo
by Emilio Rodriguez,
1976–77.

Fig. 1.15 Man and
wife planting potatoes
in snowy weather, Kiku.
Photo by John Cohen,
1964.

Maize cultivation

Maize is cultivated at lower elevations near where the jungle begins, in the area around Puskero (fig. 1.16). The Q'ero view the jungle as an irrational wilderness of endless trees. They dislike the local insect life and fear the spirits in these areas, but the maize is essential for the beer (called *axa* in the Inca language, *chicha* in Spanish) used in festivals. Some hot peppers (*uchu*), squashes, *achuq* (a fruit), and several other roots, including sweet potatoes, a New World taro, *yacon*, and *rakachu* are also grown in small quantities.

first three of these crops are used mainly as offerings in curing and fertility rituals.

The soil is poor and fields must be left fallow for five years between uses (fig. 1.14). Terracing is not used, but ditches and rocks may guide the water flow and the fields are tilled in rows parallel to the natural water drainage. Careful seed selection is practiced. The crop is stored in layers of dry *ichu* grass for ventilation. The men do most of the work of cultivation, but women help with planting and harvesting of the family's

fields (fig. 1.15). The men use an indigenous style of digging stick, now with a metal blade, to break the earth for planting.

The Q'ero cut down the wild vegetation and leave it to decay in order to prepare the fields. They do not burn it or fertilize it. In the last two or three months before the harvest, they must constantly guard against predators, including parrots and some larger animals. The maize ears are shucked and dried and the harvest is put into handwoven sacks and loaded on the backs of llamas to take it back up to the main residential areas, a two-day trip.[7] After two or three years the field must be left fallow for three years.

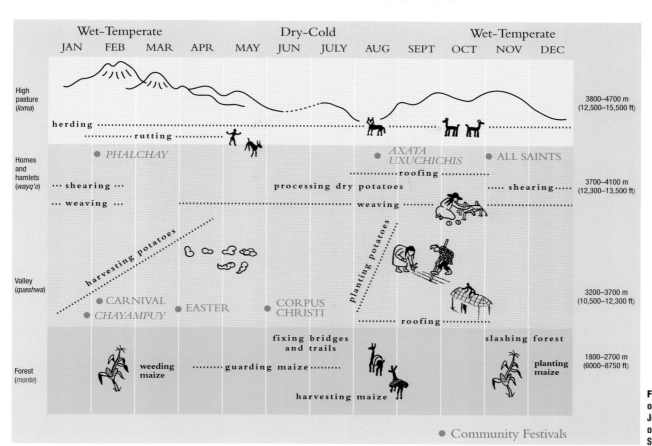

Fig. 1.17 Calendar of work. Diagram by John Cohen, based on information from Steven Webster.

Calendar

The schedule of work is complex, to balance what needs to be done at each of the elevations exploited (fig. 1.17). It also entails different family members sometimes working in different ecological zones. For this reason, larger families are an advantage.

In August through November the tuber fields are planted, the lower fields first and then the upper ones. Meanwhile, the women are watching the herds and weaving. Weaving can be done most of the year, although women are usually too busy with other things in February and March. In October is the festival of All Saints, in which the dead are remembered and conducted to the underworld. In December and January the maize is planted in the jungle, while in the high pastures, the herds are sheared. In January and February the female herd animals give birth (gestation is ten to eleven months). November through January is particularly busy for weaving in order to make new textiles for Carnival. In early February the festival to celebrate the first fruits of the potato harvest takes place and the renewal of the leadership of the community, followed by the fertility ceremony for the alpacas, and then immediately by Carnival (see Chapter 5). After the festival the rutting of the herds takes place and the harvest of the tubers begins. The harvest continues through June, again the lower fields first and then the upper ones. In late May or early June the festival of Corpus Christi is celebrated, which the Q'ero observe by sending one group of people on the pilgrimage to Qoylluriti, and another to a shrine partway down to the maize fields, with a feast on their return (see Chapter 5). Once the bitter potatoes have been harvested, the women and children process them in the high elevations in June and July, while the men go down to the forest to guard the ripening maize. Except for one person with the herds and potatoes, the whole family participates in the maize harvest in July. The fertility ceremony for the llamas takes place usually some time in August after they have brought home the maize harvest (see Chapter 5).

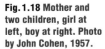

Life Cycle

At the birth of a child, an older woman outside the family helps and is given food and coca for her services. A coca offering is burned and an animal is slaughtered for food, usually by the grandparents. The parents and newborn stay home for eight days. After this period of seclusion a respected person is sought to become ritual father for the child, and the child is named. Although this ceremony involves applying water to the child's body, it is not considered a substitute for baptism, which is also done when a priest is available, though often not until much later. Infants are wrapped in a cloth secured by a belt. When children begin to toddle both sexes wear a shirt, wrap-around skirt, and knitted cap (fig. 1.18). Girls' caps do have a different design from boys', however, and a girl may wear a small shawl (*lliklla*) and a boy a poncho.

When the child is between three and six years of age, old enough to contribute to the household, the first haircutting ceremony is performed, a pre-Hispanic tradition, documented among the Incas.[8]

This ritual involves selecting another set of ritual kin. After this, gender-specific clothing is worn, and the child is given small household and herding duties, gradually learning the subsistence skills of the community. Girls and boys learn many of the same skills, although there is some emphasis on the heavier tasks for boys and on herding and household work for girls. Girls, however, also learn to weave.

Adolescence is not ritually marked. For girls, it arrives with menarche, and for boys it comes at the age of fifteen or sixteen with the ability to do adult work, at which time they also begin to use coca. The leaves are chewed with lime (*llipta*) and besides being a mild stimulant, useful for hard work at high altitudes, they are of key importance in any religious ritual (see Chapter 5).[9] At around this time the family of a youth organizes his taking of an official role in one of the community festivals. Steven Webster reports that the wearing of special textiles, particularly a patterned poncho and a vicuña scarf, is a further indication of adult social status or at least eligible bachelorhood.

At the age of eighteen or twenty young people are thinking about marriage prospects. They carry on courtships, without any stigma associated with sexual relations, while the family keeps track of each prospect's kinship and economic resources. The parents have the prerogative to approve or reject the choice of spouse. Once informal communication assures there will be no embarrassment, the young man approaches the family of the woman he is interested in with a gift of food, coca, or alcohol. Assuming this gift is accepted, the two families then meet formally to discuss such important matters as the residence of the new couple, services to be rendered, and property to be eventually inherited.[10] Usually, but not always, the couple lives with the man's family, and they provide services to both sets of parents. In most circumstances, sons inherit, with the preponderance going to the youngest, who has been taking care of his elderly parents. Women are expected to benefit from their husband's property, but they also inherit under some circumstances, such

Fig. 1.20 Man and wife
conferring about mating
llamas. Photo by
John Cohen, 1957.

as lack of siblings or if the family is wealthy. Once agreement has been reached, the couple is considered married, but there is no formal ceremony.

Since a priest rarely visits Q'ero, couples sometimes go to Paucartambo or Ocongate for Catholic sacraments, but not all are able to do this. When Steven Webster was living in Q'ero in 1969–70, people asked him to arrange for a priest to visit, and he was able to guide a Basque priest into the community to perform the wedding ceremony for many young couples at the

church in Q'ero Llaqta (fig. 1.19). The brides and grooms wore their best festival textiles for this occasion. Most of these couples had already been married in traditional terms.

Andrea Quispe Chura, of Wañuna Pampa, described the woman's role in the following terms to John Cohen (1976):

The woman's obligation – her way of living – is to attend to her husband, to help him in his work [fig. 1.20] *as well as helping her children. She is also to direct her children, and to demand that they look after the animals. Her obligation is also to spin wool and to weave ponchos, tunics, shawls, and other textiles. Women are also responsible for there being enough food prepared for their husbands and for their children.*

While the couple lives in the parents' household, the husband's father continues to hold authority for organizing the birth and haircutting rituals of grandchildren and makes sure that the husband undertakes community office. If the husband is the eldest son, he can begin thinking about separating from his father's household when his children become old

enough to help with herding (six to eight years). The division may involve the allocation of surplus resources in herds, land, household equipment, or a house, which become his inheritance.

The husband must still defer to his father, however, until he has undertaken some community leadership role as well as festival expenses, normally not until ten years or so after separating his household from that of his parents. The process of consolidating his power and influence in the community also includes strategizing for the advantageous marriage of his children.[11]

Once a couple's children start to move away, authority in everyday matters may shift to the oldest son remaining at home, but the old man's authority in ritual and political affairs increases, so long as his mental resources are intact (fig. 1.21). While men do have the titular authority, women's opinions are sought and listened to (fig. 1.20).

When a person dies, the body is normally bathed and wrapped in a purchased fabric for burial, not in the normal clothing.[12] Black purchased fabric

Fig. 1.21 Old man wearing a conservative style of poncho and cap. Photo by John Cohen, 1956.

History

Ruins of round houses and a fortification wall on a hill above Q'ero Llaqta, in a place called locally Hatun Q'ero, attest to a pre-Hispanic and pre-Inca occupation. The style of these houses is local and not Inca, suggesting a non-Inca ethnicity. The Inca occupation is, however, indicated by remains of terracing and roads, no longer in use, and occasional Inca stone implements such as mace heads. Little is known about Q'ero during the colonial period, but some of the apparent Spanish influences, such as the introduction of sheep and horses, Catholicism, and some costume elements, must date to this time.

By the mid-nineteenth century an enormous hacienda was established that included the whole Q'ero cultural area together with additional land in the Paucartambo valley, owned by the Yábar family.[14] Some plots of agricultural land were required to be cultivated by the Q'ero, with their produce turned over to the hacienda. Q'ero labor was also required in the hacienda household and in caring for European animals belonging to the hacienda. The fact that the plots cultivated for the hacienda were potato fields and not maize fields or pastures, of greater value to the Q'ero, suggests that the Q'ero nevertheless retained some control over their production.[15] Around 1920, the hacienda was divided up among several Yábar sons, with the communities associated with Q'ero Llaqta going to one of them, Benigno Yábar. During this period the running of the hacienda was not too oppressive, with the owner until the 1940s actually residing in Lima. One Yábar, who died young and did not inherit,

is used for adults, and white for children. In the case of the woman's burial recorded by John Cohen, women prepared the body. The hair of the deceased is also cut.[13] Male non-relatives, sometimes of higher status and sometimes not, perform the burial itself and prepare and serve food to the family. They are paid with hospitality and food to take home. After eight days, another ritual is performed. It appears that fine textiles are usually kept by surviving family members, though it is reported that some are buried with important leaders or ritual specialists. Steven Webster was told that the daily work clothing is disposed of separately, with care that *machu runa* (malevolent local spirits) do not get it. No weaving is done on the day that someone dies.

Fig. 1.22 Father and son with shoulder-length hair. The father is carrying a fur coca bag, Kiku. Photo by John Cohen, 1957.

was interested enough to write the first description of Q'ero, published in 1922.

The next owner, Luis Angel Yábar, was a different case, however, and people agree he was not entirely sane. He admired the Soviet revolution and tried to replicate the genetic experiments of Lysenko in his garden. He resided on the hacienda in Paucartambo and exploited the people of Q'ero with considerable avarice and cruelty. He would beat the men who were working for him as well as extracting from them more produce than had been

originally demanded, on the pretext of finding some fault. As one old man, Vernavil Machaca of Qocha Moqo, told John Cohen in 1977, "Even though we were prodded and whipped, the hacienda owners were seldom satisfied. But we still obeyed their orders." If the Q'ero resisted or tried to flee, Luis Yábar resorted to the police, who would support him. On one occasion when Yábar loaned the owner of Paucartica, a nearby hacienda, some Q'ero men as a work crew, this man forced the Q'ero men to cut their hair, which until then they had worn in a long braid, because he thought it made them look like women. This incident took place about 1940 and was traumatic since the Q'ero men regarded their hair as an important component of their pre-Hispanic heritage and identity.[16] Since then, some men have nevertheless allowed their hair to grow to about shoulder length (fig. 1.22).

The anthropological expedition led by Oscar Núñez del Prado, a professor at the University of Cuzco, in 1955 was very sympathetic to the plight of the Q'ero

under this oppressive regime. The expedition was sponsored by the Lima newspaper, *La Prensa*, which provided publicity for the abuses that were going on and helped persuade the Peruvian government to loan the community the money to buy their land from the hacienda owner, which finally took place in 1964.[17]

Since then, the potato fields that formerly were cultivated for the hacienda have been cultivated and the produce sold in order to pay off the government debt (figs. 1.23, 1.24). The cultivation work is done by the men, though women presumably help process the *moraya*. The expropriation resulted in the cessation of compulsory service at the hacienda and caring for the hacienda animals, as well as transfer of title. The Q'eros have also for the most part been able to run their own affairs. The hacienda was, nevertheless, a factor in isolating the Q'eros from the regional and national government bureaucracies and the cultural changes that were brought about in other communities by government policies.[18] For example, Luis Yábar forbade both

Fig. 1.23 Men planting the community potato fields. Photo by Emilio Rodriguez, 1976–77.

schooling and military service, which were major sources of acculturation elsewhere.

Since 1958, there has been a school in the community with a mestizo teacher. A minority of the children, those whose parents have enough other children for them to be spared from the labor needed for subsistence activities, attend for a year or so, and are taught some Spanish, the catechism, and other aspects of national culture. Since the children do not retain what Spanish they learn and the teaching includes a derogation of indigenous culture and promotion of mestizo culture, the Q'eros do not see much use in it. Instead, they have used the more cooperative teachers as cultural brokers with the outside world.[19] Thus, the influence of the school has not so far been very great. During the 1960s soccer was introduced, which the younger men are avid about, and teams among different Q'ero hamlets have been organized.

Agrarian Reform laws were passed in Peru in 1969, with the aim of breaking up many of the remaining large haciendas, although it took several years for the program to be implemented. While other indigenous communities on former haciendas were reorganized as cooperatives and supervised by government-trained engineers (not in general an improvement upon hacienda owners), Oscar Núñez del Prado was again instrumental in arranging for Q'ero to be given status as a "community," utilizing its own local governmental processes.

By the late 1970s, transistor radios began to appear in Q'ero, and so the

Fig. 1.24 Men selecting seed potatoes for the community fields. Photo by Emilio Rodriguez, 1976–77.

cooperation in his film *Carnival in Q'eros*.

In another government effort to encourage alpaca herding and increase exports, it assisted the University of Cuzco in setting up an efficiently run alpaca breeding station at La Raya, situated in the highlands between Cuzco and Puno. Because white hair can be dyed any color desired, it commands a much higher price on the international market than the browns, grays, and blacks that naturally occur in greater numbers. The emphasis on exports has caused all alpaca herders to breed for white hair. This practice is not necessarily advisable genetically, however, because it could lead to albinism in the flocks. It has also tended to make the dark hair customary for indigenous textiles less available to weavers. Thus the emphasis on white may be good for business, but it is a prime example of cultural imperialism.

The alpaca breeding station can produce greater quantities of white hair in a more efficient manner than the system used by Andean herders for thousands of years. It has the unfortunate side effect of lessening the value of alpaca hair produced by small communities such as Q'ero. So the Q'ero fiber is worth less in the market, and the net effect of this rationalized government program is to increase Q'ero poverty. Still, herding remains the central activity of Q'ero life: the focus of its economy, culture, religion, and continuity with the past.

By the mid-1990s, outside interest in Q'ero shamanism induced Q'ero ritual specialists to perform for tourists in Cuzco, as well as in Arizona and New York. In Peru, shamans met tourists at nearby sites, and a few shaman tours were led into Q'ero itself. Américo Yábar, a mestizo shaman, and to a lesser extent Núñez del Prado, also an initiated shaman, have served as intermediaries between the Q'ero and many of these outsiders, since the Q'ero shamans do not speak Spanish.[20]

Despite these influences, Q'ero subsistence so far remains much as it has always been and the Q'eros have managed to hold on to their cultural self-respect. Oscar Núñez del Prado had reported some stories about Inkarrí, a mythological figure who is seen sometimes as a culture

people became more directly aware of the world outside. Some Seventh Day Adventist missionaries came during the 1980s and are still there, having even made some converts, which has resulted in the discontinuation of the traditional religious ceremonies by those who were converted.

In recent years, the Peruvian government has instituted programs intended to help alpaca-producing communities like Q'ero by encouraging the banks to make loans to the communities or to individuals to increase their flocks. The Q'eros had

taken out such a loan, but the animals delivered by the broker were too old to produce offspring. By 1989 the debt with interest was coming due, and the Q'eros had no way to pay it. The women spoke about it this way: "They only gave us six alpacas; now they are asking for thirty alpacas"; "Now the bankers are coming to take our food"; "Now we are eating our poverty." John Cohen helped remedy this situation in 1990 by giving a herd of sixty-one fertile female white alpacas to the community in exchange for their hero and creator god, sometimes as a warrior who produced order in Andean society, and sometimes as a savior who will one day return to deliver indigenous Peruvians from mestizo domination.[21] These stories were joined with similar ones collected in other parts of Peru[22] and placed in the national Peruvian textbooks during the 1970s, encouraging a reawakened consciousness of this mythological figure among the Q'eros. In 1977, Vernavil Machaca related some Inkarrí stories to John Cohen. Although the Q'eros had always made reference to the Incas, for example, "The Incas left us here," by 1989 they identified themselves as Incas.

Inkarrí? Of what times could that have been? It is no more. However, I have heard that he walked these lands. A long time it has been since he walked this earth and they say he was powerful. So one day Inkarrí was winnowing gold, and time was running short, so he reached up and he tied down the sun. Wherever there was no water, he could grab a green snake and drag it over the mountainside and there the water would flow, even through hard rock!

Wherever there was disorder in the rocks, Inkarrí would herd them together and make beautiful walls and houses. These walls and houses would appear where he willed them to be, even though he would be on his way somewhere else. Herding the rocks with a lasso, the rocks would obey his command of their own accord. There are huge rocks in Pampaqasa. He would use those boulders in his slingshot to crumble the mountain. At the moment he was going to sling those boulders, his woman tickled him. So that is why they are still here. If the woman had not tickled him, he would have leveled down all the mountains, and the area

of Q'ero would have been flat fields. So that is the reason we have high peaks in Q'ero.

[Another time] Inkarrí was crossing the high ridges with twenty-four mules loaded with gold, and as he was coming down, the woman was coming up the river from the jungle. He said, "God willing or not, I will make my camp at the big field in Hatun Q'ero." So the woman said, "Since I am a woman, I do not have to camp where you camp, so I will camp at Qochqi [which is further down]." So the woman camped where she wished. At a place called Sachma qocha [a lake], an animal was swimming and the man [Inkarrí's muleteer] hurled stones at it. If he had not hurled stones at the animal he would have reached his destination. But as it was, he was enchanted at the lake site, and the woman arrived where she was going. These things I have heard told, so I am telling you.[23]

In 1976 a woman said to John Cohen, "We have a belief that someday a *viracocha* [white man] will come over the ridge, and he will touch us and we will die. How do I know that you are not that man?" He answered, "I've been here other times over the years, and you are still alive." There are indeed a few other outsiders, such as Oscar Núñez del Prado, who have benefited the community. But the belief quoted does have a measure of truth, since the white man's world has usually had more adverse effect upon the community than otherwise and the Q'ero are certainly justified in being suspicious of strangers.

Their textiles and music define the Q'ero identity. In the world outside Q'ero, however, they have been referred to as "dirty," "savages," as "the *ch'unchus* of the Andes," and as "sorcerers." Their music is laughed at by their neighbors. Likewise,

their wearing of a pre-Hispanic style of tunic is regarded as hopelessly old-fashioned. At a dance with their neighbors (see under *Tinkuy*, Chapter 5), John Cohen witnessed a confrontation between two men who were dressed alike. One said, "I am a gentleman from Jachacalla and you are just lowlife from Q'ero."

Once when returning to Cuzco by truck, Cohen told the mestizo driver he had just come from Q'ero. He asked, "Aren't there many Q'ero people who lie around and don't work?", "Isn't there much drunkenness?", "Don't people fight and argue a lot?", "Are there police there to keep order?", "Don't they chew coca all day?" All these questions revealed only his stereotypical views of indigenous life, since in reality they do not apply to Q'ero at all. Their relative isolation and self-sufficiency has probably been an important factor in the Q'eros' ability to persevere in their traditions in the face of this kind of ignorance and hostility. Indeed, it seemed to Webster that they have a tradition of defiance and ethnic assertiveness that many other indigenous people lack or have to a lesser extent.

Notes

1. The works of Núñez del Prado and Webster are the main published sources, of which Webster 1972a is the most detailed on daily life.

2. Webster 1972a, p. 16. Webster reports (personal communication 2000) that both the Q'eros themselves and Bette Yábar, daughter of the former owner of Kiku and Hapu, said that the Q'ero cultural area extended as far as Mollemarka. Silverman (1989, p. 38; 1998, p. 33) confirms the inclusion of K'achupata and Markachea (and K'allakancha and Pukará), but not Mollemarka. Yábar (1922) mentions Hapu, Kiku, Markachea, Pukará, and K'achupata as the main settlements, haciendas at that time. Unfortunately there are no accurate maps available that show the locations of those settlements not on our map.

3. See Rowe 1977b for more on the Pitumarka and Ch'ilka textile styles.

4. See especially Webster 1973.

5. Silverman-Proust 1988b, pp. 42–43; 1998, pp. 142, 144–45; for another alpaca and llama herding area, see Flores *et al.* 1995, vol. II, pp. 117–21.

6. Müller and Müller 1986, p. 19.

7. For further photographs, see Sekino 1984, pp. 86–90; Flores *et al.* 1995, vol. II, pp. 130–93, which documents the corn harvest in Kiku.

8. See Sekino (1984, p. 50) for photographs. Holzmann (1986, p. 196) mentions an article by Sekino published in English and Spanish, but I was unfortunately unable to locate the references as cited.

9. A detailed and beautifully written account of these aspects of Andean life in another Cuzco area community is found in Allen 1988.

10. Webster 1972a, pp. 218–58 (Chapter 7) discusses marriage negotiations and contingencies. Webster 1977 (similar to Webster 1972a, Chapter 8) discusses the kinship system and its relationship to the ecology of the region.

11. See Webster 1975 for further information on factors affecting social rank.

12. See Cohen 1979.

13. Silverman-Proust 1986b, p. 70.

14. Silverman (1998, p. 37) reports seeing an 1851 document, "Venta de la mitad de la fundio de la hacienda Markachea, Totorani y otros nombres citas … que hace Mariano Zamalloa Paz a fabor de Don Mariano Yábar." That is, "Sale of half of the property of the hacienda Markachea, Totorani, and other cited names … from Mariano Zamalloa Paz to Don Mariano Yábar."

15. Webster 1981.

16. This incident is described by Webster 1981, p. 623; Wilcox 1999, p. 253, as part of a general discussion of the abuses of the hacienda owner.
    Though certainly pre-Hispanic, such a braid is not an Inca hairstyle, since Inca men wore their hair very short (Rowe 1997, p. 29). In the anthropometric study of H. B. Ferris (1916), which does not include Q'ero, a very few of the 140 men illustrated have their hair in a long braid (pl. II, fig. 15 is clearest), although unfortunately Ferris does not make it clear where individual men are from.

17. Different aspects of this story are told by Webster 1975, pp. 152–53; 1980, p. 140; 1981, p. 624; Wilcox 1999, appendix 3.

18. Webster 1981, p. 624; Sallnow 1987, pp. 113–14; Silverman 1998, pp. 37–38.

19. Webster 1980, p. 143.

20. Wilcox 1999.

21. Núñez del Prado 1957, 1973; Morote 1958. See also Müller and Müller 1984a.

22. Arguedas 1967.

23. Translation by Jubernal Díaz. Similar stories were told to Joan Parisi Wilcox (1999, pp. 82–83).

Chapter Two Textiles and Their Uses

Fig. 2.1 Woman wearing a relatively large and conservatively styled shawl. Photo by John Cohen, 1957.

The Q'ero are inheritors of a long textile tradition, an unbroken continuity running from pre-Hispanic times to the present. Textiles are of course made for clothing, but also for a variety of other purposes including ropes, slings, bags, and carrying cloths. Most of these kinds of fabrics are made widely in the Cuzco region and surrounding areas, so we focus here on the particular variations used in Q'ero. In general, the important outer components (shawl, poncho, tunic) are of indigenous origin, as are many utilitarian textiles, although the basic garments are of Spanish derivation, probably as a result of Spanish influence during the colonial period.

Since the Inca capital was Cuzco, it might be supposed that modern Cuzco-area textiles of indigenous form could be traced directly to Inca sources, but this is not usually the case, except for some of the terminology. The Inca empire was made up of many different ethnic groups with different textile styles, only some of which have been analyzed and defined. While the Incas imposed their language on subject peoples, they did not require them to change their costumes. Fortunately Inca textiles themselves are relatively well understood,[1] so often we can say that the textile forms common today do not necessarily appear to derive from them, but probably instead derive from other pre-Hispanic styles that are less well known.

The order in which we present the textile repertoire of Q'ero parallels that of the description of the technology used in Chapter 3. The most elaborate textiles are woven by women on the indigenous four-stake loom, so these are presented first.

Women's shawls

The most important textile from an artistic standpoint is the woman's shawl (*lliklla*; figs. 2.1–2.4). It is worn in the same way as Inca examples but the modern stripe layouts and designs are different. Recent Cuzco-area shawls are made from two loom panels that are sewn together with the side edges abutting, usually with decorative stitches. They typically have outer borders in red and each panel has a central plain area in black. While in some parts of the Cuzco area, this color scheme has been modified in newer pieces (see figs. 1.6, 1.8), in Q'ero it is still strictly adhered to. Q'ero shawls are unique in having both the red and black areas composed of stripes of alternating yarn twist. Each panel of a shawl has patterned stripes on each side of the black stripe, and in Q'ero examples these often have different color combinations and sometimes design variations as well. The wider patterned stripes are in turn flanked by narrow patterned stripes of contrasting color and design. An edge binding may or may not be sewn around the outer edges. Purchased, machine-made braided wool

Fig. 2.2 Woman's shawl
collected in 1957
but probably a late
nineteenth-century
piece since it appears
to be dyed with natural
dyes. Full-figure
ch'unchu design in three-
color complementary-
warp weave. For a detail
of a very similar piece,
see fig. 3.5. 93 x 82 cm
(36⅝ x 30¼ in). The
Textile Museum 1999.7.7,
gift of John Cohen.

(or now acrylic) tape is the most common edge binding in Q'ero shawls, but occasionally a handwoven patterned edge binding is added (fig. 4.11).

The shawl is worn with the stripes horizontal across the woman's back with the upper corners pinned on the chest (fig. 2.1). Either a large needle (which may be threaded with colored thread) or a large safety pin is used to secure the corners. The use of an Inca-style silver pin with a decorative disk on one end (*tupu*), though mentioned in Luis Yábar's 1922 account, seems to have died out before 1955.[2] Q'ero shawls are small enough to be worn unfolded. A woman wears one or two shawls on a daily basis. If she is wearing two, the upper one is usually more worn and faded, presumably to preserve the lower one. For Carnival and Easter, three or four are worn at once, and the upper one is the newest and most elaborate.

The oldest shawls that have been preserved are larger than newer ones and are more finely woven, but have much

Fig. 2.3 Woman's shawl, collected in 1983. Ch'unchu design of opposing headdresses and an inti in the center, in three-color complementary-warp weave. 77 x 68 cm (30¼ x 26¾ in). The Textile Museum 1999.7.4, gift of John Cohen.

narrower patterned stripes and wider plain stripes (compare figs. 2.2 and 2.3). The increase in the size of patterned bands and decrease in fineness is typical of style change in Cuzco-area shawls in general (compare figs. 1.7 and 1.8). Some shawls that appear to be dyed with natural dyes and thus are likely to date from the late nineteenth century have been preserved in the community so people are aware of these older styles despite the fact that they are no longer worn (fig. 2.2). Many older shawls have been fan-folded perpendicular to the designs in sharp creases and were clearly stored that way. The creases are still apparent even after forty-five years of flat storage in a museum (fig. 2.4). Oscar Núñez del Prado reports that some older pieces such as this were worn as headcloths for protection from the sun, before the time when *monteras* (hats) were worn, or on certain religious occasions, for which purpose they were called *llaqolla*.[3] In the wedding recorded by Steven Webster, the brides are wearing shawls over their heads (fig. 1.19).

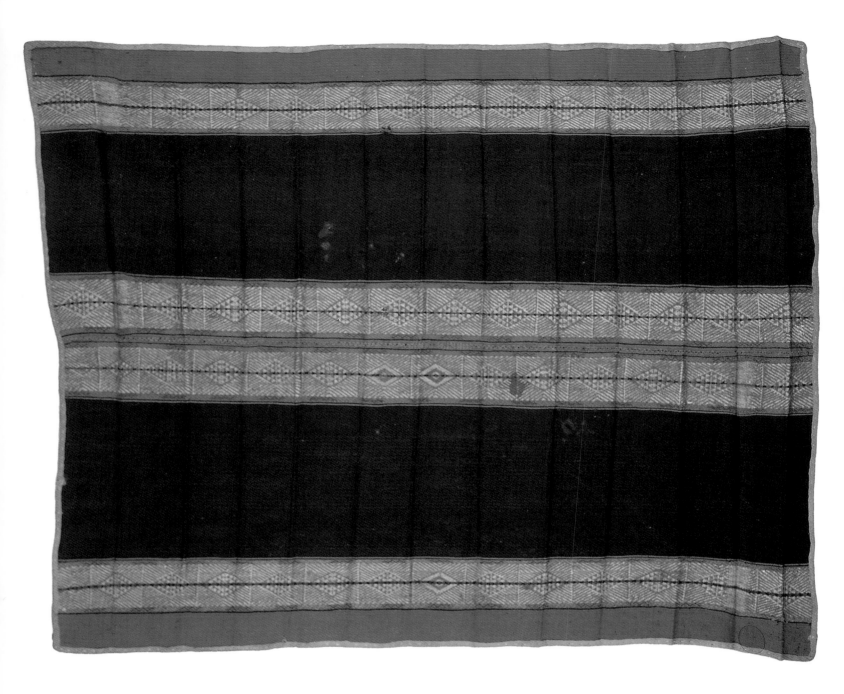

Fig. 2.4 Woman's shawl, collected in 1955. *Inti* design in supplementary-warp patterning, with sharp perpendicular creases. 86 x 69.5 cm (32⅛ x 27⅜ in). American Museum of Natural History, New York, Division of Anthropology 40.0/8888.

Fig. 2.5 Plain poncho, collected in 1964. 1.62 x 0.81 m (5 ft 3¾ in x 2 ft 8 in). The Textile Museum 1999.7.21, gift of John Cohen.

Ponchos

The poncho in its present form was probably introduced into the Cuzco area during the later part of the colonial period, although the way it is woven reflects pre-Hispanic practice. Two different kinds of ponchos are woven in Q'ero, one relatively plain (figs. 2.5, 5.1), and one heavily patterned (figs. 2.6, 2.7). Both styles are made of two loom panels and they are approximately the same size, slightly longer and narrower than is typical of ponchos elsewhere in the Cuzco area. The plain ones are usually predominantly gray or tan, but have some narrow red or pink stripes near each side edge (fig. 2.5). Usually these stripes are warp-faced plain weave, but occasionally a simple pattern is woven (fig. 5.1). There are spin stripes only near the side selvedges. The edges of the plain poncho are covered by a narrow plain-weave edge binding, which is separately woven and sewn on. Men often wear two or more ponchos at a time, presumably depending on the coldness of the weather.

Fig. 2.6 Patterned poncho, collected in 1957. Inti design in three-color complementary-warp weave with paired floats. 1.53 x 0.93 m (5 ft ¾ in x 3 ft ⅝ in) including fringe. The Textile Museum 1999.7.24, gift of John Cohen.

The patterned ponchos are called *pallay poncho*, from the pickup technique (*pallay*) used for the patterns. They have three design bands in each half, the outer two bands matching and contrasting with the center band, a typical poncho layout in the Cuzco area (fig. 2.6). The stripes between these design bands in Q'ero examples are predominantly red. As with the shawls, the plain intermediate stripes have gradually become narrower and the patterned stripes wider over time. Red and white stripes of alternating spin directions are characteristic on the outer edges, a distinctive feature of Q'ero ponchos. A separately woven fringe band is sewn along the outer edges. Q'ero men often wear an older patterned poncho underneath the plain ones on a daily basis. A new patterned poncho is worn on top of plain ones for festivals. The patterned ponchos are larger so are often not as finely woven as the shawls, but they are very beautiful all the same.

Fig. 2.7 Man wearing a poncho with inti design. The gun belongs to John Cohen's guide, Eduardo De Bary. Photo by John Cohen, 1956.

Tunics

Q'ero is one of very few places in the Cuzco area where the men still wear the pre-Hispanic style of tunic ('*unku*; fig. 2.8).[4] They also wear a shirt underneath the tunic. The tunic is black with a pink or red stripe along the outside edges.[5] Its surface is, however, enlivened by narrow stripes of contrasting directions of spin. It is made of two loom panels, sewn together leaving a central neck slit, and sewn up the sides leaving armholes. The center seam is abutted and sewn with a zigzagging stitch while the sides are laid parallel and sewn with a running stitch. The tunic usually also has an edge binding, occasionally handwoven in diamond patterns (fig. 3.28), more often machine-made braided tape, applied both up the sides and around the lower edge.[6] When men are seated, they draw their knees up under their '*unku*, which provides considerable warmth.

Fig. 2.9 Mother holding her baby wrapped with a belt, Qocha Moqo. Photo by John Cohen, 1989.

Belts

Men wear a plain-weave belt (*chumpi*) woven of undyed yarns. The belts are not unpatterned, however, since brown and white warp yarns alternate frequently in order to produce a checked design.[7] Similar belts are woven for use as waistbands on women's skirts. There are pre-Hispanic antecedents for such belts, although today they have been adapted for use with Spanish garments. The same style of belt is used to hold in place the swaddling cloth of an infant, though an infant's belt may be wider than that of an adult (fig. 2.9). The Q'ero belts are distinctive in being relatively plain; in other Cuzco-area communities, belts are often woven with figural designs in dyed colors.

Fig. 2.10 Man's bag for coca, a fine example for daily use. Inti design in three-color complementary-warp weave with single floats. 27 x 23 cm (10⅝ x 9 in). The Textile Museum 1999.7.14, gift of John Cohen.

Coca bags

The coca bag is also of pre-Hispanic origin. Two kinds of patterned coca bags are used in Q'ero. One kind is used by men on a daily basis (*wayaqa*; figs. 2.10–2.12). It can be used for carrying any small items, not only coca, and typically has a single patterned stripe down the center with plain stripes on each side. Some of the bags have coloring and designs much like patterned ponchos (fig. 2.10), while others have stripes of undyed yarn and simpler patterns (fig. 2.11). The ones like ponchos have

spin stripes along the side edges. Those of undyed yarns may have some colors of undyed yarn spun in the opposite direction to the rest. Some examples that use undyed yarns have no central patterned band (fig. 2.12). These bags have no shoulder strap and are carried by being tucked into the waistband. A number of examples have a cord at the top that can be used to tie the bag shut. A *wayaqa* is often given by a young woman to a young man as a courting gift.[8]

The second kind of coca bag is used by men for festivals (figs. 2.13–2.16). These

Fig. 2.11 Man's bag for coca, an example for daily use, collected in 1976. Side stripes of undyed yarns and Ocongate-style pattern in supplementary warp. 25 x 16.5 cm (10 x 6½ in). The Textile Museum 1999.7.15, gift of John Cohen.

Fig. 2.12 Man's bag for coca, an example for daily use without pickup patterns, collected in 1983. 24 x 18.5 cm (9½ x 7¼ in). The Textile Museum 1999.7.26, gift of John Cohen.

Fig. 2.13 Man's festival bag for coca, without pockets, collected in 1955. Side stripes with chili design in supplementary-warp, center stripe with inti design in three-color complementary-warp with paired floats. 30 x 15 cm (11¾ x 6 in), including fringe (strap missing). The Textile Museum 1974.16.20, gift of Junius B. Bird, Marion Stirling, Mary Frances Recher, and the Peruvian Research Fund.

bags are usually smaller, but have three wide patterned stripes and relatively narrow plain areas. They have a shoulder strap and are worn in matched pairs, one on each hip. Luis Yábar's 1922 report says that at that time men wore ten or twelve bags for Carnival, although only a pair is usually worn today. They are usually called *ch'uspa* (the Inca word for a man's coca bag), although Núñez del Prado also recorded the term *akullina*, which literally means "a thing for carrying coca."[9] They have an added fringe of purchased bright-red or pink sheep's wool, a kind that is especially prized and called "Castilian" wool. Usually they also have purchased braided tape sewn along the edges. The shoulder straps are either in striped plain weave or with red-and-white zigzag or chevron patterns (fig. 2.14). Some examples from around 1900 have brown vicuña-hair plain stripes (figs. 4.1, 4.22), while newer ones have red stripes.

Some of these bags have a small pocket in each stripe, called a *ñuñu* or breast (figs. 2.14–2.16). The pockets are woven on the same warp as the bag itself, in a

Fig. 2.14 Matched
pair of festival coca
bags, with six pockets,
collected in 1955.
Center with ch'unchu
design, sides with inti
design in three-color
complementary-warp
weave (paired floats).
Straps in two-color
complementary-warp
weave. 34 x 13.5–14.5 cm
(13⅜ x 5¼–5¾ in),
including fringe,
excluding strap.
Straps: 1.42 m x 8 mm
(4 ft 8 in x ⅜ in),
1.64 x 7–12 mm
(5 ft 4½ in x ⅜–½ in)
American Museum
of Natural History,
New York, Division
of Anthropology
40.0/8909 and 8910.

clever technique that has pre-Hispanic antecedents but is relatively rare elsewhere in the Cuzco area.[10] The pockets may hold the lime that is used with coca, or contain coins, but they are also decorative. The most elaborate ones have two or even three pockets in each of the three patterned stripes, although the upper pockets usually overlay the lower ones, so the total number may not be readily apparent. The examples in figs. 2.14–2.16 each have a total of six pockets; one in the American Museum of Natural History collection has nine pockets (40.0/8905), and one belonging to Steven Webster has eleven pockets.

Fur bags (*phukucho*) are also used by both men and women to carry coca and lime on a daily basis (figs. 2.17, 2.18). Oscar Núñez del Prado says that for men, this bag is made from the front part of the skin of a baby llama or alpaca, while for women it is made from the rear part (for a woman's bag, see fig. 3.6).[11] The three examples in the American Museum collection are wide below with a narrow flap above, presumably made from the neck skin. The

Fig. 2.15 Man's festival bag for coca, with six pockets, collected in 1964. Inti design in supplementary-warp patterning. 32 x 15 cm (12½ x 6 in), including fringe, excluding strap. Strap: 1.36 m x 7 mm (4 ft 5½ in x ¼ in). The Textile Museum 1999.7.13, gift of John Cohen.

Fig. 2.16 Man's festival bag for coca, with six pockets, collected in 1955. Inti design in three-color complementary-warp weave with paired floats. 28 x 13.5 cm (11 x 5¼ in), including fringe (strap missing). The Textile Museum 1974.16.19, gift of Junius B. Bird, Marion Stirling, Mary Frances Recher, and the Peruvian Research Fund.

opening is where the skin narrows. Two other narrow flaps extend downward below the opening, presumably the animal's forelegs. In the examples collected by Oscar Núñez del Prado, the opening is bound with purchased tape (fig. 2.17), while in the one collected by John Cohen the opening is not bound. These bags are also carried in the waistband.[12] Fur coca bags also have pre-Hispanic precedents, although they are uncommon today.

Fig. 2.17 Fur coca bag, collected in 1955. 39 x 21 cm (15⅜ x 8¼ in), as shown, with top folded over. American Museum of Natural History, New York, Division of Anthropology 40.0/8913.

Produce bags

Like most Andean herders, the Q'eros weave large sacks to transport goods on llama-back (fig. 1.10), and those of Q'ero are similar to the examples made and used elsewhere. Although there is an Inca word for these sacks (*cutama*), the usual word today in the Cuzco area, including Q'ero, is the Spanish word *costal*. In Q'ero these sacks are used to carry maize and potatoes to the household and to haul llama and alpaca dung down from the corrals to the potato fields for fertilizer. The bags are woven in stripes of natural colors of llama hair. Usually no two sacks have exactly the same stripe pattern, but once John Cohen witnessed a large quantity of dung being loaded onto llamas and the sacks were all the same and belonged to a single family. The bags are always sewn closed with a heavy piece of twine, which is later removed (not cut) to open the sacks. Empty bags may also be used as a ground cloth on which to lay out items for ritual use.[13] In fig. 5.4, one is used as a tablecloth.

Fig. 2.18 Group of men and women at the llama fertility festival, showing at right women's coca carrying cloths, as well as fur and woven coca bags. Photo by Emilio Rodriguez, 1976–77.

Carrying cloths

Carrying cloths, like bags, have many pre-Hispanic antecedents. They are square, and are used by placing the contents in the center, then folding two diagonally opposite corners over the contents, and then tying the remaining corners together. They are made in a variety of sizes for different kinds of goods.

In the Cuzco area women often use a small square cloth to carry their coca leaves, and Q'ero women may also use one instead of a fur bag, although examples have seldom been collected (fig. 2.18). Recent photographs show examples with narrow red-and-white stripes at the outside edges, then a few wider undyed stripes, and a patterned band in the center.[14] They also have colored corner tassels. A simpler example without dyed yarns or tassels is in the American Museum collection (40.0/8904). According to Steven Webster, these small carrying cloths are often called *wayaqa*, or if used for coca, *hallpana*.

Fig. 2.19 Carrying cloth for lunch with a dovetailed-warp join across the center, woven by Nicolasa Quispe Chura, Wañuna Pampa, collected in 1976. Warp-faced plain weave with spin stripes. 49 x 60 cm (19¼ x 23⅝ in). The Textile Museum 1999.7.10, gift of John Cohen.

A medium-sized carrying cloth is used in Q'ero to carry cold food to the fields to eat for lunch (*kharmu 'apana 'unkhuña;* figs. 2.19–2.21). *Kharmu* is eaten around 10 am during the first break from work and consists of toasted maize kernels or boiled *chuñu* (freeze-dried potatoes; fig. 2.21).[15] These cloths are a single loom panel, woven predominantly of undyed yarn, light brown on one half and dark brown on the other half, with some narrow colored stripes along the side edges (fig. 2.20). The undyed areas have stripes in alternating directions of spin.

Occasionally this type of cloth has a dovetailed-warp join through the center, creating a quartered design (fig. 2.19).[16] This technique is called *t'iklli* in Q'ero. Relatively few weavers know how to make these cloths. Textiles with dovetailed-warp joins are known from pre-Hispanic times, often with more elaborate designs.[17] Although the technique does not appear to be part of the Inca style, it was probably used in nearby highland areas about which we

Fig. 2.20 Carrying cloth for lunch, collected in 1977. Warp-faced plain weave with spin stripes. 45 x 42 cm (17¾ x 16½ in). The Textile Museum 1999.7.11, gift of John Cohen.

Fig. 2.21 Francisco Flores eating his lunch, showing the carrying cloth. At right he has two sizes of flute. Photo by Emilio Rodriguez, 1978.

have little archaeological information. Today it is rare, although it is still being used in Pitumarka.[18] In other communities such fabrics are used primarily for ritual purposes, but this is not the case in Q'ero.

Larger carrying cloths (*kana*) are woven of llama hair for carrying larger loads such as a baby.[19] Although seldom collected, those shown in photographs are in two panels sewn together, with a stripe layout similar to the woman's shawl, but the overall size is larger and they are more coarsely woven.[20] There may be a simple supplementary-warp pattern in the side stripes, but unlike the shawls the patterned stripes in each panel generally match each other. Examples without patterned stripes may divide the area that would normally be black into half black and half gray (fig. 1.24). The free corners are tied together around the shoulders of the person carrying the bundle. For a really big load, purchased fabric (*bayeta*) or simply ropes are used instead.

Fig. 2.22 Blanket.
Warp-faced plain
weave. 1.60 x 1.25 m
(5 ft 3 in x 4 ft 1¼ in).
The Textile Museum
1999.7.53, gift of
John Cohen.

Blankets

A large coarsely spun and woven blanket of undyed llama hair in two loom panels is used for sleeping, or to sit upon (fig. 2.22). Like the produce bags, they usually have stripes in several undyed colors, and sometimes have patterns made using narrow stripes in different colors similar to the belts. Blankets in other Cuzco-area communities are often more colorful.

Certain kinds of textiles are made predominantly by men, using a variety of techniques. Some of these techniques are ancient (braiding for ropes and slings), while others are European introductions (knitting).

Ropes

Men braid ropes (*waskha*) using coarse yarn spun from undyed llama hair in a variety of colors. They are used to tie loads to the backs of llamas as well as to secure larger loads to people. Like the produce sacks, similar rope is made in all herding communities in the southern Peruvian highlands. Men in Q'ero may also wrap a rope around the waist as a belt over their tunic or ponchos when they are working.[21] In addition, women use them to tie the loom bars to the stakes to maintain the tension on the warp when weaving (see Chapter 3). A man gives a fine rope for a loom to a woman he is courting.[22]

Fig. 2.23 Braided dance sling for Corpus Christi, collected in 1957. Length: 1.80 m (5 ft 9⅛ in). Cradle width: 4.5 cm (1¾ in). American Museum of Natural History, New York, Division of Anthropology 40.1/2279.

Slings

Slings (*waraqa*) are used mainly in herding, to scare off predators and to guide the animals. They can fling stones accurately over long distances. Slings in this part of the Andes have a central tapestry-woven cradle with a cord on each end made of undyed llama hair using fancy braiding techniques. A stone is placed in the cradle, the two ends of the cords are held in the hand, and the whole device is whirled in a circle to gain momentum, and then the end of one cord is released, which releases the stone.

More elaborate slings are made to wear wrapped diagonally around the body in dances. Some dancers for the pilgrimage to Qoylluriti (see Chapter 5) wear a sling with a large end tassel (fig. 2.23).[23] A sling with multiple tassels suspended from it is worn tied under each arm and over the shoulder for dances at the *Phalchay* ceremony and Carnival (fig. 2.24).[24] The tassels, in intense reds and blues, of purchased "Castilian" wool, are attached to narrow braids that are suspended from the sling along at least one third of its

length. The braids are connected to each other with cords at intervals, running parallel to the sling. The tassels are thus more prominent than the sling. The dyed yarns in the braid of the example shown are not typical for the period.

Fig. 2.24 Dance sling for Carnival, collected in 1957. Length of tassels: 64 cm (25¼ in), length of sling: 1.60 m (5 ft 3 in). American Museum of Natural History, New York, Division of Anthropology 40.1/2280.

Fig. 2.25 Girl wearing a knitted cap with representational figures. Photo by John Cohen, 1956.

Caps

Q'ero men knit caps (*ch'ullu*) to wear themselves, as well as for children of both sexes (figs. 2.25–2.28). The caps are worn at all times, rarely removed. Indeed, they are emblematic of a person's indigenous status. Although knitting is a European introduction and the term *ch'ullu* is not found in the earliest Inca dictionaries, similar caps may have been worn in some areas in pre-Hispanic times. Knitted caps are now worn throughout the southern Andes.[25]

The style worn by young girls in Q'ero is distinctive: dark brown or black with a red or orange diamond grid (fig. 2.25).[26] Some girls' caps have a ruffle or flap on the front. Occasionally they may have animal or other single motifs, usually embroidered. The example in fig. 2.25 has a llama, cross, plow, and bird on the center front diamond, seemingly emblematic of life in Q'ero.

The designs on the hats worn by men and boys resemble those on hats from the Ocongate area, and many Q'ero hats are

Fig. 2.26 Knitted caps with undyed yarns, collected in 1955. The left one is for a boy, the right for a man. Left: 61 x 20 cm (24 x 8 in). Right: 66 x 21.5 cm (26 x 8½ in), including tassels. The Textile Museum 1974.16.16 and 17, gift of Junius B. Bird, Marion Stirling, Mary Frances Recher, and the Peruvian Research Fund.

Fig. 2.27 Man's knitted
cap with dyed yarns,
collected in 1957.
52 x 23 cm (20½ x 9 in).
The Textile Museum
1999.7.18, gift of
John Cohen.

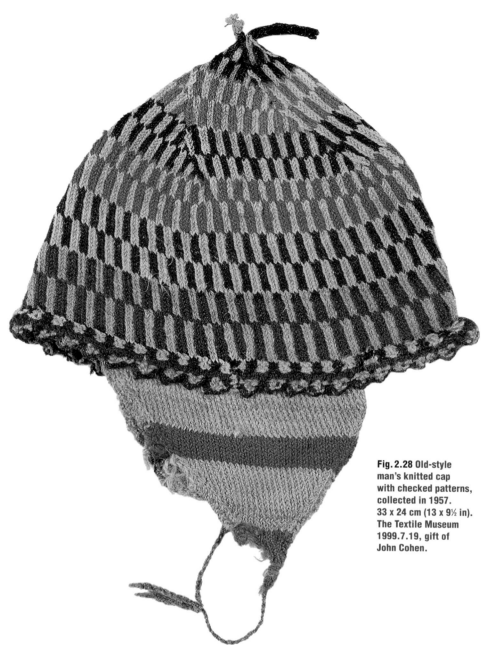

Fig. 2.28 Old-style
man's knitted cap
with checked patterns,
collected in 1957.
33 x 24 cm (13 x 9½ in).
The Textile Museum
1999.7.19, gift of
John Cohen.

indistinguishable from those of neighboring areas. The earliest photograph of a Q'ero man, dating from the 1910s or early 1920s, shows a hat of this style (fig. 4.7). The older style caps are made of undyed camelid hair yarns (fig. 2.26), but most modern examples are made from brightly colored purchased yarns, either of sheep's wool or acrylic (fig. 2.27). Newer examples are also often decorated with white seed beads and buttons.

One hat collected by John Cohen, however, has a design of stripes in natural colors of yarn, and this may represent a late example of a yet older style (fig. 2.28). Photographs from the 1950s show similar examples worn by old men (fig. 1.21).

Small knitted bags worn by the lead llama in a llama caravan have also been reported.[27]

Fig. 2.29 Saddlebags, collected in 1957. Warp-faced plain weave with embroidered pile. The side shown: 41 x 39 cm (16 x 15⅜ in). American Museum of Natural History, New York, Division of Anthropology 40.1/2187.

Fig. 2.30 Horse blanket, collected in 1957. Warp-faced plain weave with embroidered pile. Overall: 98 x 54 cm (38½ x 21¼ in), excluding fringe. American Museum of Natural History, New York, Division of Anthropology 40.1/2184.

Saddlebags and horse blankets

Saddlebags are used to carry food when traveling, either on foot or on horseback (fig. 2.29).[28] This form is a Spanish introduction and not usual in the Cuzco area though it is found elsewhere in the Andes. Q'ero saddlebags consist of two coarse bags woven of undyed llama hair joined by separately woven narrow bands. The surface of the bag is embroidered with geometric designs in brightly colored pile. Bags with similar embroidery occur but are rare in the Cuzco area.

A related textile is used as a horse blanket on festive occasions (fig. 2.30).[29] This is a larger loom panel of undyed cloth with widely spaced rows of long, dark pile fringe, embroidered in the same way as the bags but with longer monochrome pile. The pile hangs downward from the middle, that is, changing direction in the middle. Such horse blankets have not been reported from elsewhere in the Cuzco area.

Fig. 2.31 Men's festival scarves. Warp-faced plain weave with spin stripes. Widths: 18, 19, 22 cm (7, 7½, 8⅝ in). The Textile Museum 1974.16.101 and 102, gift of Junius B. Bird, Marion Stirling, Mary Frances Recher, and the Peruvian Research Fund. 1999.7.20, gift of John Cohen.

Festival scarf

The scarf is also a Spanish introduction, worn in a few other Cuzco-area communities. Q'ero men formerly wore scarves made predominantly of brown camelid fiber, with spin stripes and three evenly spaced groups of colored stripes (fig. 2.31). The scarves have four selvedges with a bright-red or pink wool fringe added to each end, of the kind typical on festival bags and dance slings. Although Oscar Núñez del Prado says they are called *panoylo* (from Spanish *pañuelo*), Steven Webster says that *chalina* (another Spanish loan word) is the usual term in Q'ero, as elsewhere. Núñez del Prado also says they are woven of vicuña hair.[30] The vicuña is a wild relative of alpacas and llamas that has even finer hair. The tawny brown color of these scarves is certainly that characteristic of vicuña hair, though the colored stripes may be alpaca hair. The oldest Textile Museum example (fig. 2.31 left) is indeed probably vicuña hair; its dyed stripes appear to have been coloured with natural dyes, which may indicate a late nineteenth-century date (the fringe is clearly newer than the weaving). Steven Webster also has one that is extraordinarily finely woven, with some twenty spin stripes in each of the brown stripes. Two newer Textile Museum examples (fig. 2.31 center and right) are probably made of alpaca hair, however, and the newest one has more colored stripes and fewer undyed stripes than the older examples.

In 1970 Steven Webster was told that men spun and wove these scarves, although he never actually saw this being done. Q'ero men also said that they still corral or corner vicuña in the mountain valley heads (between the alpaca pastures and the glaciers), and then shear them and set them free. They say they never kill the animals, since they are spirits of alpacas that are reborn in the herds. At that time some Q'ero men wore such scarves at festivals and other ceremonial occasions. They were felt to look dashing, especially worn for horseback riding. Even then, however, many men were wearing white knitted (machine-made) scarves instead, and more recent festival photographs show only the machine-made examples.

Khipus

During the hacienda era, the few Q'ero men who were in charge of keeping track of the produce demanded of the community by the hacienda owner still spun yarns to make *khipus*, which were used to keep these numerical accounts.[31] These were simplified versions of the similar accounting devices used by the Incas. They consisted of a series of different natural and dyed color yarns that had knots tied in them. Small knots represented ones, medium knots tens, and large knots hundreds. The different colors represented the different items counted. There was no code that specified what color was used for what item. The man simply used the cords to help him remember the numbers.

Fig. 2.32 Boy's shirt
(aymilla), collected in
1955. 33 x 67 cm
(13 x 26⅜ in), including
sleeves. American
Museum of Natural
History, New York,
Division of Anthropology
40.0/8894.

Spanish garments from purchased fabrics

Other clothing items are made from
purchased fabric. The most common such
fabric is what is called *bayeta* in the Cuzco
area, a Spanish word referring to a coarsely
woven wool fabric; the term becomes *ch'i
wayta* in Q'ero.[32] This fabric is coarsely
handspun and handwoven by men on
Spanish-style treadle looms, in either plain
weave or twill. Q'eros purchase the cloth
either from itinerant merchants or in the
markets of Ocongate or Paucartambo.
Men in Q'ero cut and sew the garments
by hand. The garments, like the cloth,
are of Spanish origin, probably dating
from the later part of the colonial period.

Men, women, and children all wear
a simple kind of shirt, called *aymilla*
(a Spanish word; fig. 2.32). This garment
is an interesting contrast to the white
shirts and blouses plus vest and/or
jacket traditional in other Cuzco-area
communities. The style is a pullover,
with a V-neck, no collar, and long
sleeves. Black, dark brown, and red are
common colors. The ends of the sleeves
are typically trimmed with a kind of

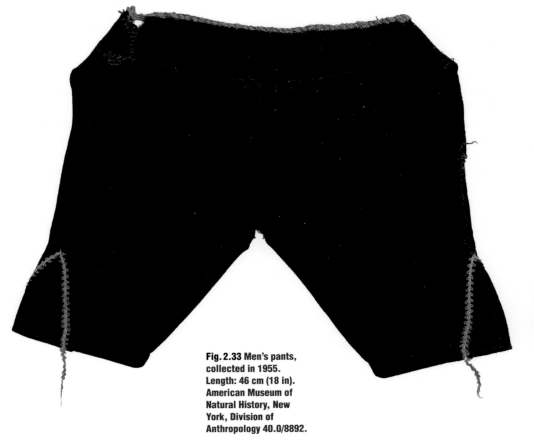

Fig. 2.33 Men's pants,
collected in 1955.
Length: 46 cm (18 in).
American Museum of
Natural History, New
York, Division of
Anthropology 40.0/8892.

Fig. 2.34 (opposite)
Women wearing
monteras. They are
preparing ichu grass for
thatch (cf. fig. 1.13).
Photo by John Cohen,
1956.

purchased tape that is common in the
Cuzco area. It is also handwoven on
Spanish-style treadle looms and called
kolón (from the Spanish *golón*).[33] The tape
has diamond patterns in twill weave and
weft stripes that are made by tie-dyeing
the weft before it is wound on the
bobbins for weaving.[34]

Women also wear full skirts (*pollera*, a
Spanish word) that are pleated into a
waistband, similar to those worn elsewhere
in the Cuzco area.[35] The skirts are black,
and have their lower edges trimmed either
with purchased *kolón* or with a locally
woven band called *luyru*. These bands also
have diamond twill patterns woven with
a white warp and a red or striped weft.
Q'ero women wear the skirts to just
below the knee in length. They wear two
or three skirts at once, for warmth, and
more for festivals.

Small children of both sexes wear a
wrap-around skirt (*phali*) made of *bayeta*
until they are toilet-trained, similar to
elsewhere in the Cuzco area.

Men wear knee-length pants (*kalsona*,
from the Spanish *calzón*), often made not
from *bayeta* but from a machine-made
black fabric (Spanish *bayetón*; fig. 2.33).[36]
The exact length is variable in the Cuzco
area, but in Q'ero it is just above the knee,
probably derived from eighteenth-century
European costume. The pants in fig. 2.33
have small triangular gussets at the knee,
whose seams have a trim consisting of a
pink rick-rack like tape. The pants have
an alpaca-hair cord to secure the waist,
but men also use a handwoven belt.

Some men and women at festivals wear
a red or green waist-length jacket (*jubón*,
a Spanish word) with button trim on the

sleeves, similar to those worn elsewhere
in the Cuzco area.[37] They are also made
from machine-made fabric.

Women also wear a kind of round, flat
hat called a *montera* (a Spanish word),
made with a coiled grass foundation,
covered with black fabric on top and red
under the brim, and with added trim of
various kinds (fig. 2.34). Different Cuzco-
area communities use different shapes of
montera. The *montera*, like the *ch'ullu*, is
emblematic of indigenous status (fig. 2.35).
Those worn in Q'ero are made there by a

Fig. 2.35 Cairn (used
as a marker and to
scare off predators)
resembling a woman
wearing a montera.
Photo by John Cohen,
1957.

person who specializes in them. The Q'ero shape is relatively wide and flat with a small center peak, trimmed with purchased tape woven of metallic thread. The tape is sewn around the upper outer edge, and quarters the top except for a central circle. Frequently women also wear flowers on their hats. Although formerly women wore the *montera* daily, now they are more likely to wear a felt fedora-style hat, and to keep the *montera* mainly for festivals. Festival *monteras* have colored streamers hanging down over each ear, some handwoven and some of purchased braided, or sometimes flowered, tape (fig. 5.14).[38] Further colored paper ribbons may also be added.

Before about 1940 men also wore *monteras*, but since then men have worn felt fedoras over their knitted *ch'ullus* when walking.[39] An exception is found in certain male officials at Carnival, who wear a *montera* with waist-length machine-woven flowered ribbons.[40] Some women living in hamlets near Ocongate have recently started to wear the style of *montera* characteristic of the Ocongate

area.[41] This style has a slightly smaller diameter, no trim on top, and fabric hanging down over the edge with colored fringe along the bottom.

In anticipation of death, each person has their own burial cloth ready. For an adult it is a dark-blue or black *bayeta* fabric and it is sewn during the preparation for burial. A woman John Cohen knew whose baby was sick said "Let's kill our little white alpaca to make a stew." Alas, the baby died, and shortly afterwards she too got sick and died. From her *bayeta* funeral cloth they cut her burial gown, using the hair of the little white alpaca to make yarn to sew the garment together.[42]

Purchased items

Comparatively few clothing items are purchased, acquired either from itinerant merchants or in regional markets. The felt hats mentioned above are one example, however. They appear usually to be acquired at second or third hand, and frequently have a hatband made with supplementary-weft patterning that is also purchased. Like *monteras*, women often decorate them with flowers.

All men and most women own sandals made with tire treads, a product used by indigenous people throughout the Cuzco area. They are worn mostly for traveling. When Oscar Núñez del Prado first went to Q'ero in 1955, he found three men who still wore an older style of sandal (*seq'o*), made from the rawhide of the neck of a llama, just as Bernabé Cobo reports was the case for Inca sandals.[43] These were locally made.

Although in 1970 people wore machine-made clothing items only for festivals, soccer games, or in jest, many now wear machine-made shirts and sweaters either in addition to or instead of the *bayeta aymilla*, and a few men also may wear purchased machine-made long pants. Purchased scarves have also been mentioned above.

Notes

1. Rowe 1997.

2. Yábar 1986, p. 192.

3. Two pieces collected for the American Museum of Natural History in New York are described as llaqolla: 40.0/8887 and 8888 (fig. 2.4). See also Núñez del Prado 1968, p. 246; Flores *et al.* (eds.) 1984, pp. 18, 115; Flores and Fries 1989, p. 26.

4. Silverman (1998, p. 58) says that tunics are also worn in Asaroma and Quichu in the heights of Markapata, not very far from Q'ero.

5. Besides those illustrated, The Textile Museum has another example given by John Cohen (1999.7.22, collected in 1964). It has pink tape edge binding but the edge stripes are red.

6. The American Museum of Natural History has a boy's tunic without edge binding (40.0/8890) and a man's with a handwoven edge binding (40.0/8891), collected in 1955 by Oscar Núñez del Prado.

7. A rather tattered example is in the American Museum of Natural History collection 40.0/8915. See also Müller and Müller 1986, p. 179 (showing a baby) and p. 199 (showing an older boy).

8. Webster 1972a, p. 218; Núñez del Prado in Flores *et al.* (eds.) 1984, p. 119.

9. Núñez del Prado's American Museum of Natural History accession list, 40.0/8905-8911.

10. For a description of how this type of pocket is woven in Tarabuco, Bolivia, see Cason and Cahlander 1976, pp. 154–59. The technique in Q'ero is probably similar.

11. The American Museum of Natural History accession list, 40.0/8912, says a young llama was used; in Núñez del Prado 1968, p. 252; Flores *et al.* (eds.) 1984, p. 23 he specifies young alpaca.

12. Webster 1972a, p. 193.

13. See, for example, Müller and Müller 1986, p. 123.

14. This description is based on the photos in Sekino 1984, pp. 30–31, 50 bottom, 92 lower left. Although at least some of these cloths have Ocon_gate-area designs, and Ocon_gate-area coca carrying cloths have a similar format to these Q'ero examples, the Ocon_gate-area ones have asymmetrically colored undyed stripes, while the Q'ero ones are symmetrically colored.

15. Núñez del Prado in Flores *et al.* (eds.) 1984, p. 19.

16. Another example, of virtually identical color layout, though slightly larger (67 × 61 cm/ 26 × 24 in), was collected by the archaeologist Percy Paz, who had interpreted for Ann Pollard Rowe in 1974, and gave the piece to her. It had been woven in 1990 by a woman in Kiku.

17. For a discussion of pre-Hispanic examples, see Rowe 1977a, Chapter 6, and fig. 44.

18. Thanks in large part to the efforts of Nilda Callañaupa and the Center for Traditional Textiles of Cusco, affiliated with Cultural Survival. For examples, see Rowe 1977a, p. 29, fig. 19, from Checacupe, a town near Pitumarka whose textile style is similar; Mercado 1995; Meisch (ed.) 1997, p. 116, cat. 170. These carrying cloths are larger than those from Q'ero and often have patterned stripes. Elayne Zorn (1986, p. 297; 1987, pp. 512–13) has also reported smaller examples from Macusani in the Department of Puno. The Textile Museum has another small example purchased in Chinchero in 1980, but probably from the Urubamba or Lares area (1991.41.2).

19. The term *kana* for a carrying cloth was recorded by Webster 1972a, p. 92.

20. Sekino 1984, pp. 33, 68, 87; Flores *et al.* 1995, vol. II, pp. 141, 149, 154.

21. Sekino 1984, pp. 64, 65, 66; Müller and Müller 1986, p. 79.

22. Núñez del Prado in Flores *et al.* (eds.) 1984, p. 119.

23. For a photo of a man wearing a sling, see Silverman 1998, p. 158, fig. 7.8.

24. For photos of men wearing these slings, see Flores *et al.* 1995, vol. II, pp. 239, 244. Local terminology is given by Silverman (1988b, p. 40; 1998, p. 137). Silverman 1998, fig. 6.5 is a back view, showing its construction. The support for this recent example is not described as a sling, but rather a wider braided band.

25. See LeCount 1990.

26. There is one in the American Museum of Natural History's Núñez del Prado collection (40.0/8896). See also Sekino 1984, pp. 30, 68, 69, 73, 87, 95.

27. Silverman 1989, p. 16; 1998, pp. 59, 69.

28. Núñez del Prado's American Museum of Natural History accession list, 40.0/8889, which

also has a diamond design. A third example in the American Museum is 41.0/2186, which has a vertical and horizontal grid design.

29. John Cohen also collected another very similar example for the American Museum of Natural History (40.1/2185).

30. American Museum of Natural History accession list, 40.0/8898, which does indeed appear to be woven with vicuña hair. See also Yábar (1986 [1922] p. 191), who says that "a large number" of vicuña scarves were worn for Carnival.

31. Cohen 1957. Núñez del Prado 1950 discusses some similar *khipus* from communities between Q'ero and Paucartambo, although it is not completely clear what the cultural affiliation of these communities is.

32. The term is found in Núñez del Prado's American Museum of Natural History accession list, 40.0/8893, an *aymilla*.

33. See previous note.

34. See Rowe 1977a, pp. 23–24.

35. Silverman 1998, p. 58, gives the term *aksu*, the Inca word for a woman's wrapped dress, for these skirts.

36. Núñez del Prado's American Museum of Natural History accession list, 40.0/8892.

37. Sekino 1984, pp. 97, 98; Müller and Müller 1986, pp. 121, 126; Flores *et al.* 1995, vol. II, pp. 154, 235, 238, 239, 244, 248. The term is from Yábar 1968 [1922], p. 191. He says the jacket is worn over the *'unku*, which seems doubtful.

38. See also the photos in Sekino 1984, p. 98 lower left; Müller and Müller 1986, p. 121; Flores *et al.* 1995, vol. II, p. 241.

39. Webster 1972a, p. 49 (note 1). Yábar (1968, pp. 192) in his description of Carnival costume of 1922, says that men wore *monteras*, while women wore ribbons hanging from their hair.

40. Flores *et al.* 1995, vol. II, pp. 239, 244, 245.

41. See the photographs in Sekino 1984, pp. 72 top, 95 center bottom; Silverman 1988a, fig. 26; Silverman 1991, fig. 32; Silverman 1994, fig. 2. The Silverman photos were taken in 1985.

42. See Cohen 1979.

43. Núñez del Prado 1968, p. 252; in Flores *et al.* (eds.) 1984, p. 22; also the American Museum of Natural History accession list 40.0/8914.

Chapter Three
Making Textiles

In Q'ero nobody specializes only in weaving. Everyone spins and makes fabrics as a part of normal living, and family matters take precedence over weaving. A woman known to John Cohen had progressed only a little more than a centimeter (less than half an inch) on a fine shawl from one year to the next. In a community where everyone weaves, it is natural that some women have more talent than others, and some enjoy weaving more than others. A woman who has both of these gifts, like Nicolasa Quispe Chura, may set challenges for herself and produce fabrics that are truly exceptional, which some might consider works of art. The people of Q'ero acknowledge these fine fabrics; in fact they can often recognize a weaver's identity by her work.

Textiles are made by the family for their own use. Although shirts, skirts, and pants are made from purchased fabric, many other items are handspun and handwoven using aboriginal techniques. This textile technology is enormously time-consuming and requires a significant level of skill, but the resulting fabrics are of great complexity and beauty. All such fabrics made in the home are personalized. That is, they are made with a particular person and often a particular circumstance in mind.

When people make something for their own use in an economy that is based on subsistence rather than money, they can invest however much time and trouble they might wish to. When they are making something to wear at a festival or for someone that they love, they often put in the extra effort to make it especially beautiful.

This situation is completely different from our own culture, where time is

money and things have to be made in the quickest and cheapest manner. Even before industrialization, most fabric was made in Europe on a commercial basis, not only in professional workshops but also by women at home. This difference in economy and attitude is exemplified in the following conversation with Martina Quispe Apasa in Qocha Moqo, recorded by John Cohen in 1976. He asks, "Would you let us buy the beautiful shawl you are making, along with the loom?" The weaver answers, "No, it would be like asking me to sell you my arm." Cohen tries again, "But you could make another shawl. People in my country would like to see your beautiful work. They would appreciate the weavers of Q'ero. It would be admired by many people on the walls of a museum." She answers, "What is a museum? I'm not making this for sale. This shawl is for my daughter." Of course he then desisted. Cohen also recorded the intense delight of a little girl putting on a new shawl for the first time in his *Peruvian Weaving* film (1980).

Q'ero children learn textile skills as they are growing up, by watching and helping their parents or other adult relatives and then by practicing on their own. Younger children also learn from older ones.[1] By working with their parents in this way, children learn the skills they need to maintain their culture once they are grown. It is a kind of learning different from that used in schools, but it is learning nonetheless. John Cohen asked Andrea Quispe Chura (Nicolasa's sister) of Wañuna Pampa to tell him about when she first learned to do the pickup patterns and she answered, "Who can remember such time when I was just a young girl running barefoot in the world. The mestizos spend their time learning to read and write, while we spend our lives perfecting our weaving."

Before beginning a weaving, a woman makes an offering of maize beer to Pachamama, or Mother Earth.

The locally woven textiles are warp-faced and warp-patterned, which is typical of contemporary weaving in south highland Peru and Bolivia. The warp is the set of yarns that is initially put on the loom before the actual weaving, or

Fig. 3.1 Woman spinning. The yarn has already been dyed. The paper streamers on her hat are for Carnival. Photo by John Cohen, 1957.

Fig. 3.2 Man spinning yarn in a community meeting. Photo by Emilio Rodriguez, 1976–77.

Spinning

Alpaca hair is used for clothing, while llama hair is woven into blankets, carrying cloths, and produce bags, and braided into ropes and slings. Sheep's wool is used only occasionally. This wool has surface scales that make it scratchy and easy to spin. It is these scales, which are also responsible for the tendency of wool to felt, that justify a sheep's fleece being called "wool" rather than hair. Alpaca hair and llama hair have far fewer scales and those they have are faint, so that the fiber is much softer to the touch, as well as more difficult to spin. Alpaca hair is stronger but less stretchy, having less natural crimp, than sheep's wool.[2] Spinning it very tightly, as is done in the Cuzco area, gives the yarn enough elasticity as well as strength to make weaving warp-faced cloth feasible. Alpaca hair is also considerably warmer than sheep's wool because, except for the finest hairs, it has a hollow core that traps air.

Alpacas are shorn once a year during the milder part of the wet season (January), using a steel blade sharpened on a rock. Each animal may, however, be shorn only once every two years for a yield of longer fibers. The chest of the females and the stomach of the males are left unshorn, which is thought to protect them from exposure.[3] A male yields more than 2.25 kg (5 lbs), and a female about 1.8 kg (4 lbs) of fiber. The length of the fiber is usually 10–20 cm (4–8 in).

Both girls and boys learn to spin, and everyone contributes thread to the household, although women spend more time spinning than men (fig. 3.1). Hand spinning is slow, and it takes much longer to spin the yarn for a fabric than it does to

insertion of the weft, takes place. "Warp-faced" means that the warp yarns are more closely spaced than the weft, and so they visually predominate in the fabric. The weft yarns are hidden. "Warp-patterned" means that the visible pattern is formed by the warp yarns.

Fig. 3.3 Nicolasa Quispe Chura plying yarn. Photo by Emilio Rodriguez, 1976–77.

weave it. Thus people are spinning any time they are not doing some other work with their hands. In a men's meeting to discuss political issues, most of the men keep their hands busy by spinning or knitting (fig. 3.2). Old people spin when they can no longer do heavier labor.

All yarn is spun for a specific purpose. That is, the spinner knows exactly what kind of textile the yarn she is making will be used for. Warp yarn must be spun more tightly than weft yarn, because it is held under tension on the loom. Yarn for

a woman's shawl is spun more finely than that for a produce sack. Because of these variations in yarn size and twist, and other variables, it can take more or less time to spin a given length of yarn. The number of interruptions will also of course affect the amount of time spinning takes. As an average, however, a rate of a little over one meter (about three feet) per minute is typical in spinning with a hand spindle, with a maximum of double this amount.[4]

Most of the yarn used in locally woven textiles is spun on a hand spindle using hair from the spinner's own animals (figs. 3.1–3.2). There are two possible directions in which fibers or yarns can be twisted, one corresponding to the central part of the letter "S" and the other to the central part of the letter "Z," so they are called S-twist and Z-twist respectively. Plying, or twisting two (or more) spun yarns together, produces a yarn that is more even and stronger than spinning alone (fig. 3.3). The plying is normally done in the opposite direction to the spinning so that the two directions

Fig. 3.4 Detail of a scarf showing stripes of S-plied and Z-plied yarns. The brown stripe is 2.5 cm (1 in) wide and has seventeen spin stripes. The Textile Museum 1974.16.102, gift of Junius B. Bird, Marion Stirling, Mary Frances Recher, and the Peruvian Research Fund.

reinforce each other. In Q'ero a plied yarn is a metaphor for the interdependence of a married couple.[5]

In south highland Peru, the typical yarn is Z-spun and S-plied, which is called *paña*, or "right." Yarns spun and plied in the opposite direction are called *lloq'e*, or "left." *Paña* and *lloq'e* are also philosophically contrasting concepts in Andean belief and ritual. The definition of these concepts is complex and partially dependent on context but, for example, *paña* is the path to the world of spirit (communication with supernatural beings) and is considered more masculine, while *lloq'e* is the path through which one accesses practical magic, such as healing or divination, and is considered more feminine. Thus *lloq'e* yarns are believed to have special powers in the Cuzco area.[6] For example in Q'ero, such yarns may be worn on the wrists or ankles as a protective device and are wrapped around injured or diseased parts of the body as a component of the curing ritual, after which the yarns are disposed of in the river.[7]

Q'ero textiles are notable for having stripes of alternating twist in the plain-weave areas (fig. 3.4). Six warp yarns of each direction are typical, though four or eight are also found. Although this feature can be found in some other textiles from southern Peru, particularly in older examples from more remote areas, it is usually confined to the outer edges of the piece. In Q'ero, however, the entire plain-weave areas of shawls, tunics, scarves, and carrying cloths for lunch are covered with spin stripes. Sometimes the yarn of different directions of spin is also from two different animals, so that these stripes are also slightly different colors, making them easier to see.

The Q'eros give a number of explanations for using stripes with opposite directions of spin. Some are practical. For example, they say that these stripes prevent the edges from curling, which is why the stripes are often found at the outside edges of a piece even when not used elsewhere. Such fabrics are also believed to shed water better. Other explanations are metaphorical. The stripes keep opposing forces in balance. They are also recognized as one of the identifying characteristics of Q'ero textiles.

To spin, the fiber is first teased apart with the fingers and then loosely rolled so that the roll can be wound around (or draped over) the left wrist. The hair (or later the newly spun thread) is attached to the top of the spindle with a slip knot. Holding the spindle in her right hand, the spinner rubs the tip between her fingers, in a motion like that used to snap the fingers (for Z-twist), or between her hands, moving the right hand away and the left hand toward the body (for S-twist), in order to set the spindle spinning.[8] Once it is twirling the spindle may be dropped, but when the spinner is seated, the bottom tip of the spindle rests on the ground (fig. 3.2). While the spindle is twirling, the spinner draws out the fibers with her hands to form the thread. When the yarn is as long as she can reach with her arms outspread, the spinner winds the thread onto the spindle, after which the process is repeated. This is a general description. Some spinners may hold the spindle in the hand while doing the initial drafting of the fibers (fig. 3.1). The first motions are often more of pulling out the fiber, and subsequent ones more of twisting it. Some spinners wind the yarn onto the fingers of the left hand before winding it onto the spindle. To ply yarn, the two threads to be combined are wound together into a ball (called doubling), which then may be pinned to the skirt, and the spindle is used to twist them together, using the same motions as for spinning (fig. 3.3).

Dyes

Synthetic dyes have been in use for the last hundred years or so and are obtained at the Ocongate market, other regional markets, or from itinerant indigenous traders who come to the community with llama caravans of goods to sell. Synthetic dyes are much easier to use than natural dyes, and are relatively inexpensive. Nevertheless, in the period from 1955 to 1970 older people still remembered something about natural dye plants growing within the community's territory, and some of the plants are known as dye plants elsewhere in highland Peru as well (figs. 3.4, 3.5).

For red, the root of *chapi* was used.[9] Elsewhere in the Peruvian highlands the word *chapi* refers to one of various species of *Relbunium* or *Galium*, in the same family as madder, an Old World red root dye. These plants have been a source of red from early pre-Hispanic times. It is interesting that no one has recorded a recollection in Q'ero of cochineal, a red insect dye, which was used for red in other parts of the Cuzco area. *Ch'ilka*, a yellow

dye, has been identified elsewhere as *Baccharis lanceolata*, *B. polyantha*, or *B. prostata*. It is not clear which of these plants, or another presumably related one, the Q'ero term *hatun ch'ilka* might refer to. *K'uchu k'uchu* for dark green or black, identified elsewhere as *Baccharis genistelloides*, and *cheqchi* for yellow or green, identified elsewhere as *Berberis boliviana*, *B. carinata*, or *B. rariflora*, have also been recorded. The name *waqra-waqra*, yielding a brilliant yellow dye, may also refer to *Berberis boliviana*. All these plants are known elsewhere as good for dyeing. The other plants mentioned cannot at present be identified.[10]

John Cohen reports that the Q'eros were also familiar with *añil* (the Spanish word for indigo), which they would probably have obtained in the past by trade with indigenous itinerant merchants from the Puno area. He was also told of urine being used with a dye, probably indigo, and also of lemon as a mordant, although lemons are a Spanish introduction and would presumably have to have been purchased. A mordant helps the dye to form a chemical bond with the fiber. Another mordant mentioned was *qolpa*, a word that seems to refer generally to soils with mineral content, for example copper sulfate, which is a good mordant. Cohen was told of two types, one for blue and the other for red. Dyeing may be done before spinning, as suggested by the photograph fig. 3.1.

Fig. 3.5 Detail of a shawl with old *ch'unchu* design, dyed with natural dyes, in three-color complementary-warp weave. Width of *ch'unchu* design band: 3 cm (1¼ in) each. The Textile Museum 1974.16.117, gift of Junius B. Bird, Marion Stirling, Mary Frances Recher, and the Peruvian Research Fund.

The four-stake loom

Women use the indigenous four-stake loom to create four-selvedged fabrics (fig. 3.6). In this loom the two loom bars are each tied to a pair of stakes that have been pounded into the ground. This style of loom is typical of the southern part of the Cuzco area, as well as of the department of Puno and the adjacent areas of northern Bolivia. North of the Cuzco area the backstrap loom is more typical. Women's shawls, men's tunics and ponchos, as well as bags, carrying cloths, and blankets, are woven on the four-stake loom. Most weaving takes place out-of-doors on the patio in front of the house, but in bad weather it may be done inside by the open door, which is the only source of light.

Although most woven cloth has side selvedges where the weft yarns turn after being put between the warp yarns, the making of end selvedges is not so common. It is, however, a characteristic of indigenous weaving throughout the Americas. It is a completely different way of thinking about cloth production from the European tradition in which long lengths of fabric are woven and then cut up to make shaped garments and all the raw edges have to be hemmed. People who go to the trouble of making a four-selvedged fabric are naturally disinclined to cut it. Instead, textiles are made to the exact size wanted, and the garments are all rectangular. To make a larger textile than can be conveniently woven in one piece, such as a woman's shawl or a man's poncho, two fabrics are sewn together edge to edge, usually with decorative stitching. The pattern on such a fabric is created on the loom during the weaving process, with the layout of the finished garment in mind. It is not added afterwards.

Making a four-selvedged cloth obviously entails not cutting the warp at any point during the weaving. The warp yarns are not tied to the loom bars, but rather the end loops of the warp (held by the heading cord, or first weft) are secured to the loom bars using a separate cord. The devices used to raise and lower the warp yarns in order to insert the weft are put on without cutting the warp and can be removed likewise. Generally the weaver

Fig. 3.6 Loom for a poncho panel with *ch'unchu* designs in three-color complementary-warp weave, showing the heddle rod controlling the colored threads and the shed rod the white threads. The pattern stripes pass around an additional stick at the end of the loom. The weaver is taking coca from a fur bag and has *phalcha* flowers on her hat. Photo by John Cohen, 1957.

Fig. 3.7 Detail of a
shawl by Nicolasa
Quispe Chura of Wañuna
Pampa. The pattern has
been woven throughout
the terminal area. See
full view fig. 4.14.
Maximum loom width:
31.5 cm (12½ in). The
Textile Museum
1999.7.2, gift of
John Cohen.

weaves a distance from one end, and then turns the warp around in order to weave from the other end. When the distance between the two woven ends of the cloth becomes so short that the devices that raise and lower the warp threads cannot be used, these devices must be removed. The remaining weft yarns are darned in with a long needle, a process that takes much longer than normal weaving. This section is called the termination area. It is typical of Cuzco-area weaving that on textiles where two panels are sewn together, the termination areas of each panel are placed at opposite ends of the piece.

In a warp-faced and warp-patterned textile, it is very difficult to insert these last few weft yarns so that the pattern is not broken. In Q'ero textiles there may be two centimeters (less than one inch) or so that lacks a pattern. Often the weaver crosses the warp yarns in the patterned stripes in order to make narrow warp stripes (fig. 3.16). If she did not do this rearrangement, this section would have horizontal banding or be mottled. Q'ero weavers frequently use a design in the short area on the other side of the termination that is different from the rest of the textile. It is the mark of an especially fine weaver if she does attempt to match the pattern. The shawl of Nicolasa Quispe Chura is exceptional in this respect (fig. 3.7). She not only continued the pattern throughout the termination area, but also attempted to match the design where the weaving from the two ends met, a feat in which she was remarkably successful.

The principle of pattern weaving is also different in most indigenous American weaving from that used on European-style treadle looms. In European looms (except for tapestry looms) the loom mechanism normally creates the designs. Thus, it takes more time to put the warp on the loom initially, but then the cloth can often be woven nearly as fast as if it were plain. In indigenous American looms on the other hand, usually only the basic mechanism for plain weave is applied, so that if patterns are wanted, the weaver has to select the desired warp yarns by hand before passing each weft, called "pickup" in English or *pallay* in the Cuzco area. The principle is similar to that of tapestry weaving. This is of course much more time-consuming, but at the same time a relatively complex pattern can be produced on simple equipment and the weaver also has the option of varying the designs as she goes along. This reliance on hand picking is a key reason for the artistic excellence of Peruvian weaving. The patterns are memorized and consist of components that can be repeated, reversed, or inverted.[11]

Fig. 3.8 A husband assists his wife in warping a shawl. The first half has already been woven and is seen at the lower left of the photograph. Photo by John Cohen, 1957.

Warping

To put the warp (*'allwi*) on the four-stake loom of the Cuzco area, a loom bar (*'awa k'aspi*) is first tied to each pair of stakes (*takarpu*), using braided llama hair ropes (fig. 3.8).[12] A cord of measured length may be used to set the distance.[13] The weaver sits at one end of the loom, while an assistant (another adult family member) sits at the other end. They toss each ball of yarn back and forth in sequence, making a figure eight around the two loom bars, usually working left to right (fig. 3.8).

The assistant also helps by adjusting the spacing and tension of the yarns at their end. The weaver counts the warp yarns very carefully, since they will form the stripes in the finished warp-faced cloth. To add a new color she lays the end of the new yarn under the previously warped ones next to the warping bar. If two yarns alternate frequently, they are simply carried next to the warping bar when not used and become incorporated into the weaving parallel to the heading cord (first weft). The balls of yarn to be used rest on the ground next to the front loom bar, their ends caught next to the loom bar under the warp threads that have been already wound (fig. 3.9). The weaver picks up a ball from this group to use, and when finished puts it back, to exchange for another. Colors used only in the borders are not carried across the entire warp at the loom bar, however.

For plain weave the shed rod (*tokoro*, a kind of cane used for this purpose), a lightweight stick of relatively large diameter, is inserted into the opening behind the cross of the figure eight. The heddles (*'illawa*) are thread loops that pass around the warp yarns in front of the warping cross and around the heddle rod, a narrow stick that rests on top of the warp. It is the alternating use of the shed rod and heddle rod that creates plain weave. There is also a narrow lease stick (*murmuna*) behind the shed rod, under the same warp yarns controlled by the heddle rod, holding an additional warp cross (fig. 3.11). This stick is not actually manipulated but simply helps to hold the warp yarns in position. Other Cuzco-area weavers may not employ such a lease stick, but it is usual in Q'ero.

Another stick, the sword (*khallwa*), is used to bring each new cross forward, hold the warp yarns apart while the weft yarn is inserted between them, and to beat down the weft. In most areas, the sword has a flattened shape, with a profile somewhat like an airplane wing. In Q'ero, however, it has a relatively round cross-section. Usually only one sword is used, but sometimes two (figs. 3.10, 3.11). A final tool (*ruk'i*), usually called a "pick" in English, is a stick with a point at one end, made from wood or a camelid leg bone.

Fig. 3.9 Nicolasa Quispe Chura and her mother warping the dovetailed-warp carrying cloth, showing how the balls of yarn are handled to change colors. A white thread is lying along the loom bar, and will be picked up again in the border. Also visible here is Nicolasa's shawl now in The Textile Museum collection (fig. 3.7). Photo by Emilio Rodriguez, 1977.

It is used both to select warp yarns in pattern weaving and to help beat down the new weft yarns. For extra fine cloth, a thinner pick is used.

To make the heddles, the weaver first inserts the sword into the opening. She then puts the thread that will be used to make the heddle loops through the opening from right to left, with the ball remaining at the right side of the loom. She makes the first loop on the left by tying it to size. Then working from left to right she picks up the string between each

warp yarn and wraps it around a finger of her left hand from front to back, making a spiral. The weaver puts the heddle rod through the loops when there are too many to hold on her finger. When the loops are finished, she ties off the thread on both ends of the heddle rod.

The weaver then ties the front loom bar to the warp. First she places a heading cord that will be used in the first weft passes through the opening in front of the cross. Then she places the loom bar on top of the warp and ties the heading cord

loosely to both ends. With a second cord the weaver lashes the warp and the heading cord to the loom bar in a spiral motion and ties it loosely at both ends. She then tightens the lashing, afterwards tying it firmly. Next she lifts the warping bar away from her up over the stakes, and brings the loom bar towards her and ties it to the stakes. The warping bar can then be removed. The weaver may then adjust the warp spacing and the actual weaving can begin. Usually the first two or three weft yarns are a heavier cord than the weft in the rest of the textile (fig. 3.12).

To lift the yarns controlled by the shed rod, the weaver brings the shed rod close to the heddle rod, holds them at both ends and pulls them back and forth a few times. She may also drag the point of the pick across the warp. When the yarns are separated she inserts the sword into the opening formed in front of the shed rod. The ends of the heading cord are then inserted into this shed and this weft is beaten down. To beat, the weaver brings the sword as close as possible to the loom bar, and beats the pick across it in successive motions over the width of the warp. This motion makes a distinctive clattering noise that advertises to anyone nearby that weaving is going on. To lift the yarns controlled by the heddle rod, the weaver moves the shed rod away from the heddle rod, so she can lift the heddle rod with her left hand and punch down the warp behind the heddle rod with her right fist (fig. 3.13). The sword is inserted, and she may then bring the cross forward with her fingers and the pick (fig. 3.14). Then the weft (*mini*) is put through and beaten down in the same manner as before.

Fig. 3.11 (top) A produce sack on the loom, showing the arrangement for weaving warp-faced plain weave. The weaver is using two swords, the front one not sword-shaped. With her right hand she holds the bone pick to beat with. Photo by John Cohen, 1957.

Fig. 3.12 Inserting the first weft into the shed-rod shed. Photo by John Cohen, 1957.

Fig. 3.13 (above)
Punching down the
warp in order to lift the
heddle rod. The weaver
has draped an old cloth
over the far end of the
warp to keep it clean.
Photo by John Cohen,
1957.

Fig. 3.14 The weaver
has inserted the sword
in the heddle-rod shed
and is bringing the cross
forward with her fingers
and the pick. Photo by
John Cohen, 1957.

Complementary-warp weave

The principle of complementary-warp weave is that there are at least two sets of warp, usually of different colors, that are co-equal in the fabric.[14] In the most basic form, one color interlaces over three (creating a three-span float), then under one weft, while the other color interlaces in the reverse of this pattern, under three, then over one weft. When the fabric is warp-faced, the warp yarns are more closely spaced than the weft so the weft is hidden. Thus, the three-span floats of one color predominate on one face of the fabric, while the floats of the other color predominate on the reverse. The two colors can be exchanged from one face of the fabric to the other to create patterns. The floats on each face can be aligned with each other in various ways. The unusual, rather coarsely woven bag shown in fig. 3.15 has the floats aligned in alternate pairs.

The most common patterning technique in Q'ero women's shawls, men's ponchos, and coca bags is a type of three-color complementary-warp weave in which white is opposed to two other colors, such as pink and navy or red and black. Despite the use of three colors, the designs are completely double-faced, registering equally clearly on both faces of the fabric. Remarkably enough, this structure has not so far been discovered in pre-Hispanic Peruvian textiles. Inca textiles with three-color complementary-warp patterning are not double-faced.[15] The technique therefore appears to be a post-Conquest invention, but one that appears to owe nothing to Spanish influence. It is indeed an indication that the Peruvian weavers of recent generations are as inventive as their ancestors. The technique is used not only in Q'ero but also in the Pitumarka and Lares areas, although only in Q'ero is it common to interchange all three colors within a single design rather than changing faces only along horizontal lines between designs. The Q'ero technique is of course more virtuosic.

In this structure (fig. 3.16), the white is usually forming a three-span warp float on one face of the fabric (interlacing over three weft yarns), while one of the other colors is forming a corresponding

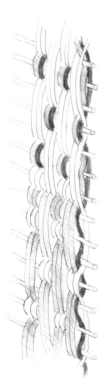

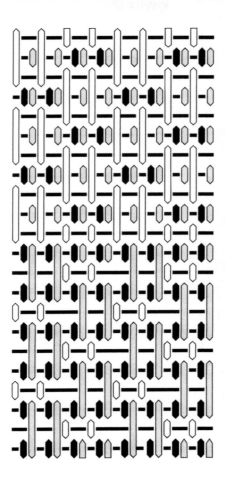

Fig. 3.16 Diagrams showing three-color complementary-warp weave, with 1/1 interlacing used to hide the third color. Both show alternating warp order and three-span floats aligned in alternate pairs, as is typical in weaving *ch'unchu* designs. Left: Drawing by John Cohen. Right: Diagram by Ann Pollard Rowe.

Fig. 3.17 Detail of a shawl with three-color complementary-warp weave patterned bands with alternating warp order. The main design is *ch'unchu* but *inti* has been woven in the terminal area. Width of patterned stripes: 7 cm (2¾ in). The Textile Museum 1993.18.28, gift of Sylvia Helen Forman.

three-span warp float on the opposite face (interlacing under the same three weft yarns). The third color meanwhile interlaces over-one, under-one, and is thus hidden by the two floats in a warp-faced fabric. In the basic form of this structure (fig. 3.16), seen most clearly in the *ch'unchu* designs (fig. 3.17, frontispiece), especially the older ones (fig. 3.5), the floating warp yarns interlace over-three, under-one. The three-span floats are aligned in alternate pairs, as with the two-color example illustrated (fig. 3.15).

Diagonals have floats overlapping by one weft yarn. The colors alternate regularly, white, color, white, color. The stepped diamond design, *qocha*, is often woven in the same way (figs. 4.19–4.20).

The *inti* designs (figs. 3.18–3.20), however, have the yarns changing faces after each float so the white interlaces over-three, under-three. In the diagonals, the three-span floats overlap alternately by two weft yarns and by one. When the overlap is two weft yarns, the warp order changes, so that two whites or two colored

Fig. 3.18 Diagrams showing three-color complementary-warp weave, with 1/1 interlacing used to hide the third color. Both show interrupted alternations typical for weaving *inti* patterns. Left: Floats aligned in alternate pairs. Right: Floats alternating singly. Drawing by Ann Pollard Rowe.

Fig. 3.19 Detail of a poncho with *inti* design in three-color complementary-warp weave with paired floats. Width of the patterned band: 3.5 cm (1⅜ in). The Textile Museum 1981.9.37, gift of Marion Stirling Pugh.

floats are adjacent. The warp thus has to be set up with the particular design in mind. These seemingly subtle refinements produce a more elegant design, as can be seen by comparing an *inti* woven in a shawl that was set up to produce predominantly *ch'unchu* designs (fig. 3.17). There are two styles of weaving *inti*, one in which the floats are in alternate pairs (figs. 3.18 left, 3.19), and one in which they alternate singly (figs. 3.18 right, 3.20). The latter is probably more time-consuming to weave, but produces a more finely detailed design.

The arrangement of shed rod, heddle rod, and lease stick is similar to that used for plain weave, but with one third of the warp (white) controlled by one device and two thirds (both colors) by the other (instead of half-and-half). So in warping, one white warp forms half of the cross while two differently colored yarns together form the other half. An extra stick, called a *k'espa*, is sometimes placed under the patterned stripes at the far end of the loom next to the back loom bar (fig. 3.6). A weaver told John Cohen that

Fig. 3.20 Coca bag with *inti* design in three-color complementary-warp weave with single floats. 32 x 29 cm (12⅝ x 11⅜ in).

The Textile Museum 1974.16.99, gift of Junius B. Bird, Marion Stirling, Mary Frances Recher, and the Peruvian Research Fund.

Fig. 3.21 Loom for a coca bag with *ch'unchu* designs in three-color complementary-warp weave. The heddle rod controls the white threads, and the shed rod the colored threads. The weaver is opening the shed-rod shed. Photo by Emilio Rodriguez, 1976–77.

Fig. 3.22 Two women weaving shawls and one spinning (right). The woman in the center has the white yarns and colored yarns controlled by different devices in order to create a design in which these threads change position in the center. The woman at left is weaving with the white yarns over the shed rod, and the colored yarns on the heddle rod. Photo by John Cohen, 1957.

Fig. 3.23 Loom for a shawl panel, with the warp colors mixed on the heddle rod and shed rod, probably for weaving *inti* designs. Photo by John Cohen, 1957.

this stick was to separate the patterned stripes from the plain areas. We have not encountered this extra stick used elsewhere in the Cuzco area.[16]

In Q'ero there is no consistency about which threads are controlled by the shed rod and heddle rod. For weaving *ch'unchu* designs the white threads of the complementary-warp weave may be controlled by the heddle rod, while the other two colors both pass over the shed rod (fig. 3.21), or these positions may be reversed (fig. 3.22). If the heddles control the colors, a warp of each color passes through the same heddle loop.[17] For weaving *inti* patterns some white and some colored threads are controlled by each device, due to the altered warp order (fig. 3.23). Since the weaver selects which colors will be lifted entirely by hand, any of these methods of setting up the warp will work equally well. Cohen timed one weaver at about eight minutes to pass a single weft element, although this will of course vary according to the width and fineness of the design.

Supplementary-warp patterning

In a minority of Q'ero textiles, the typical Cuzco-area supplementary-warp technique is used, either instead of complementary-warp weave or in addition to it (figs. 3.24, 3.25). This supplementary-warp technique does not appear to be of great antiquity in the Cuzco area although some examples probably from the late nineteenth century are known.[18] It is significantly easier to weave than the three-color complementary-warp weave and it appears that it has been gradually replacing the use of complementary-warp weave in some areas.[19] In the Ocongate area, it is used in all the warp-patterned textiles and has been since at least the 1940s; an older style in this area is unknown. In Pitumarka and Ch'ilka, it is used alongside both two-color and three-color complementary-warp weave (fig. 1.8).

In this structure the supplementary-warp yarns float on one side of the fabric to create a design and then on the opposite face between design areas. The designs are made up of small shapes so that the supplementary-warp floats correspond to the length of these shapes and seldom span more than five weft yarns. In Q'ero-style textiles the supplementary warp is usually pink, orange, or red, while the ground warp is white. The weft is commonly black and is visible in the finished textile in flecks where it passes over the ground warp and supplementary warp at the same time (fig. 3.25).

The designs specific to Q'ero, such as the rayed diamond (*inti*) and zigzags formed by small triangles (figs. 4.13, 4.17, 4.18, 4.22, 4.23), have been carefully composed so that the shapes formed by the floats are the same on both faces, producing a textile that does not have a right or wrong side. In recent years, however, some weavers have begun to use Ocongate-area designs, which do have a right and wrong side (figs. 4.24, 4.25).

Regardless of the designs woven, the structure has a ratio of two ground-warp yarns for each supplementary-warp yarn, but the ground-warp yarns are paired, with the supplementary-warp yarn changing faces in the middle of each pair

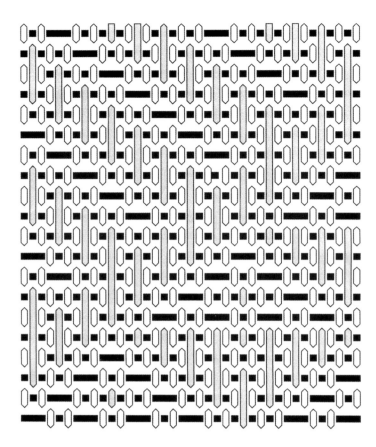

Fig. 3.24 Diagram of plain weave with supplementary-warp patterning. Drawing by Ann Pollard Rowe.

Fig. 3.25 Detail of a shawl with *inti* design in plain weave with supplementary-warp patterning. Width of supplementary-warp patterned stripe: 8 cm (3⅛ in). For a full view see fig. 4.13. The Textile Museum 1974.16.87, gift of Junius B. Bird, Marion Stirling, Mary Frances Recher, and the Peruvian Research Fund.

(fig. 3.24). This result is brought about by an ingenious arrangement of the heddles. The heddles are applied to alternate warp yarns (and the shed rod passed under the remaining yarns) regardless of whether they are supplementary-warp or ground-warp: á a é a á e á a é a á e, and so on.[20] When weaving, each supplementary-warp yarn is either picked up (*pallay*) to create a pattern float on the upper surface or depressed to float on the back, leaving the paired-warp plain-weave ground to form naturally. Sometimes the ground-warp yarns are also floated in narrow diagonal lines for patterning purposes (fig. 4.23). Ground-warp floats also occur behind narrow horizontal lines of supplementary-warp pattern.

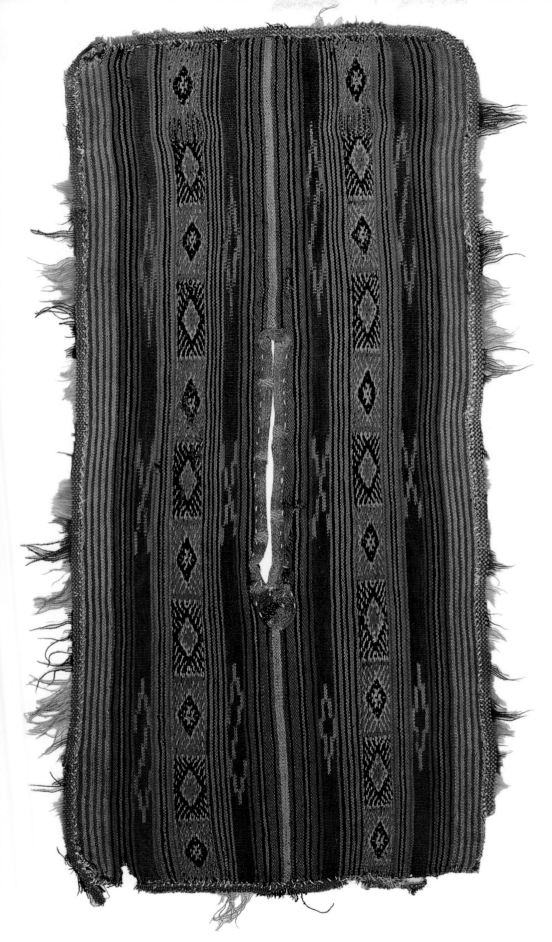

Fig. 3.26 Boy's poncho
with warp-resist dyed
patterns and *inti*
design in three-color
complementary-warp
weave with single floats
(except some pairing in
the centers). 99 x 51 cm
(39 x 20 in), including
fringe. The Textile
Museum 1974.16.100,
gift of Junius B. Bird,
Marion Stirling, Mary
Frances Recher, and the
Peruvian Research Fund.

Warp-resist dyeing (warp *ikat*)

Although no longer being done at the
time of John Cohen's first visit to Q'ero
in 1956, warp-resist dyed stripes are found
on some older ponchos (figs. 1.21, 3.26,
4.5). The designs are simple ones, stepped
S-shapes, X-shapes, and diamonds. The
technique has continued to be used in
other parts of the Cuzco area, most
notably in the Q'atqa-Kauri area, adjacent
to the Ocongate-style area.[21] It is usually
specific to ponchos and was probably
introduced along with the poncho during
the later colonial period.

In this technique, the warp yarns for
the resist-dyed stripes are first warped
separately from the others. Then groups
of warp yarns are tightly wrapped with
another yarn in those areas that will
form the design. From the available
Q'ero examples, it appears that the warp
was tied at full length and that each stripe
was tied separately. The wrapped yarns are
then immersed in the dye bath. The dye
does not penetrate the yarns under the
wrappings, which thus "resist" the dye.
After dyeing, the ties are removed. The
warping is then done for the full poncho,
one panel at a time, incorporating the
resist-dyed yarns, and weaving proceeds
as usual.

Dovetailed-warp color changes

In the late 1970s John Cohen noticed a small carrying cloth that although a single textile appeared to be four complete smaller cloths joined together, so he inquired about it (fig. 2.19). What was it for? How was it done? Who did it? At first the Q'ero men did not appear to acknowledge that it was exceptional, but eventually they told him that it was made by Nicolasa Quispe Chura in Wañuna Pampa. A man explained about Q'ero weavers, "Where there is curiosity, they can weave anything."

Cohen already knew the weaver and that her fabrics were exceptionally fine, so he asked her about this textile. She said she did not have any yarn prepared so she could not show him how it was done. He begged her to prepare the yarn, so that he could return the following year to film the process. A year later she had many excuses why it could not be done. She was very pregnant, due to give birth soon, and once more her husband was not around. Furthermore, she needed her mother to help set up the warp and the mother was away in the potato fields helping her husband with the planting. Eventually, however, the mother arrived and he was able to document the warping of this fabric.[22]

To create the discontinuous-warp join in the center, an extra loom bar is used in the center, tied to two additional stakes (figs. 3.9, 3.27). First the lower half of the textile is completely warped, in a figure eight, just like a regular textile. Then the upper half is warped. The yarns of the first half are spread apart with the fingers in order to fit the ball of yarn between them. To put the work away, after the warping is completed, the warp is rolled from each end to the center. Each section is woven like a larger piece, first from one end and then from the other. A yarn is substituted for the central warping bar when the warp is turned to begin weaving from the center of the textile.

Belts and bands

For a narrow warp, for example to make belts and bag straps, only one stake is used, and the other end is secured to the weaver's waist with a needle. For weaving short and even narrower bands such as hat ties, the weaver may use her big toe instead of a stake.[23] The heddles may not be tied to a stick but may be just looped together with thread, and instead of a shed rod, a loop of yarn is usually used. One of two structures may be used. Belts and some bag straps for festival coca bags are simply warp-faced plain weave, with warp stripes to make the surface interesting. When two colors of warp yarn alternate, one is controlled by the heddles and the other by the shed loop. Thus lifting them alternately produces narrow horizontal stripes of alternating colors. This same principle can be used to create checks.

The other structure found in festival coca-bag straps is a two-color complementary-warp weave (fig. 2.14). The two colors are warped alternately, often red and white. When one color is floating on one face of the fabric, the other color is floating on the back. Usually simple designs such as chevrons and diamonds are used. John Cohen's weaving film shows a coarser band in two-color complementary-warp weave being woven with a black-and-white diamond pattern (based on a diamond-twill weave). For this simple design, three sets of heddle loops are used along with the shed loop, and pickup is not needed.

Fig. 3.28 Detail of a tunic with handwoven edge binding. Length of arm-hole: 19 cm (7½ in). The Textile Museum 1999.7.23, gift of John Cohen.

Skirt borders

Both men and women weave skirt borders. The warp is set up as for a warp-faced band but the warp is plain white and not as closely spaced. It is the weft that is colored and creates the design. The weave is usually some kind of diamond twill. In twill weaves, the yarns float over two or three of the opposite set, and the floats are lined up diagonally. These weaves are created by using multiple sets of heddles. The weft is usually red (sometimes striped), and does not completely cover the warp, which makes the diamond designs show more clearly.

Twill is rare among surviving pre-Hispanic textiles, and definitely an oddity in the Cuzco-area textile repertoire. Its association with women's skirts, which are obviously of Spanish derivation, makes colonial introduction a possibility. The technique could well have been devised by Andean weavers attempting to imitate Spanish treadle-loom woven trimming bands.

In other parts of the Cuzco area, these bands are woven with loop heddles similar to those used for other belts and bands, but in Q'ero a type of heddle introduced from Europe is used, that elsewhere in the Cuzco area is used mainly for poncho borders. The hole-and-slot heddle is made from a row of slats of bamboo with a hole in the middle of each slat, tied together at the top and bottom. For plain weave, as is usual in poncho borders, the warp yarns pass alternately through the spaces between the slats and through the holes. The heddle is lifted for one shed and lowered for the alternate shed. Since twill weaves require multiple sheds, however, Q'ero weavers use up to four such heddles.[25]

Edge bindings

Many Q'ero textiles have no special edge bindings, while others simply have a length of machine-made braided tape sewn to the edges. A few textiles, however, have a more elaborate handwoven edge binding, typically with a diamond design (fig. 3.28). One tunic and one shawl in The Textile Museum collection have such an edge binding. The dark weft of these bands is threaded on a needle so that it can be put through the cloth as the band is being woven rather than weaving it separately and sewing it on afterwards. The edge binding has eight monochrome warp yarns in warp-faced plain weave on each side (red in the tunic, green in the shawl). The diamonds are also basically warp-faced plain weave interlacing but the colors not in use float on the inside where they are not visible, in a kind of warp substitution.[24] The exception is the white yarn on each side of the central diamond, which interlaces over-two, under-one throughout.

Fig. 3.29 Weaving
bayeta on a four-stake
loom, Wañuna Pampa.
Photo by John Cohen,
1977.

Other weaving

Although the Q'ero style is closely pre-
scribed and distinctive, Q'ero weavers do
of course have the skill to weave anything
they happen to require. One weaver of
Cohen's acquaintance needed some *bayeta*
cloth, but could not get to the Ocongate
market and in any case had no money to
buy it. Instead she spun coarser yarn of
looser twist to duplicate that used for *bayeta*,
and set up her four-stake loom to weave
more widely spaced warp yarns to duplicate
the effect of treadle-loom weaving (fig. 3.29).

Men's textiles

Although women do most of the
weaving, there are certain kinds of
textiles that are made by men. Some
of these techniques are a continuation
of an indigenous tradition while others
are Spanish introductions.

The braiding of ropes and slings is an
indigenous tradition dating well before
the Spanish conquest, and still practiced
throughout the central Andes in all the
herding areas.[26] In order to make coarse
llama-hair yarns for this purpose, men
use a distinctive spinning technique. The
man holds the fiber in his left hand and a
stick in his right hand and rotates his right
wrist to impart twist to the fibers.[27] The
stick used may be relatively thick, and
John Cohen saw one man using his flute
for this purpose.

Ropes are braided similar to making
a pigtail, bringing each yarn from the
outside to the center, but usually seven
strands are used instead of three, and five
or nine strands are also possible. Ropes
are nearly always striped in natural colors;
using four colors in a single rope is not
uncommon.

More complicated braids are made for
slings that have a four-sided structure. The
maker holds the base of the braid in his
fist, with the unused yarns hanging down
loosely from the top.[28] He takes one yarn
from each of two opposite sides of the
braid, twists them and lowers them on
one side where they are held down by
the fingers. Then he takes the adjacent
pair and lowers them on the opposite side
from the first. After doing this with all the
pairs from the same two sides, he rotates
the braid and does the same with the pairs
from the other two sides. Using variations
of this technique, a large variety of color
patterns can be produced. The most
elaborate examples have a central core of
additional yarns, from which color
substitutions can be made.

In Q'ero slings, usually one handle of
the sling is a fancy braid of this kind,
while the other handle is a simpler braid,
made more like a rope. The loop is made
near the end of the fancy braid by
dividing the yarns into two groups,
braiding each group separately, and then

recombining them. The cradle of the braid is made using a slit tapestry weave, a variant of weft-faced plain weave in which the weft passes back and forth only in its own color area. The maker creates a narrow warp similar to that used for other narrow bands, but does the weft-faced interlacing without the aid of heddles, leaving a slit in the middle to help hold the stone.

Knitting on the other hand, used to make the caps that men and children wear, is a European introduction, probably dating to the colonial period.[29] The techniques used in the Cuzco area have a number of features no longer used in Europe and presumably represent an older European tradition. The caps are made in the round on five needles, each with a fine hook on one end. The yarn is carried around the neck and thrown with the left hand. The knitters work on the inside of the hat, so they are actually purling.

Men also hand sew the Spanish-style garments made from *bayeta* or machine-made fabric. Although most clothing is made within the family and not purchased, one person in the community specializes in making *monteras* (women's hats), and in 1970 a crippled man was making articles of clothing to exchange for labor in his fields.[30]

The pile embroidery on saddlebags and horse blankets is also done by men, presumably because these accouterments are also colonial imports. The pile is most often sewn as if it were a cow hitch (two symmetrical loops), with two vertical stitches appearing on the back of the fabric and a crossbar with the two ends on the front. Sometimes it is sewn with two stitches forming a simple upside-down U-shape, or with the loop of the "U" pulled down so it passes under the pile ends (making a cow hitch that is the reverse of the most common stitch).

Treadle-loom weaving

Weaving on Spanish-style treadle looms seems not to have been done in Q'ero in the last fifty years. John Cohen photographed one disused loom in Q'ero in 1957, however, so it may possibly have been done sometime in the past. This type of loom is used elsewhere in the Cuzco area to weave the *bayeta* fabric used in Spanish-style garments. Since weaving on treadle looms was a commercial activity done by men in Spain, the same is true in its Andean incarnation.

Here it is sufficient to point out only the general principles of how this loom works, to emphasize how different it is from the indigenous Andean style of loom. The loom has bars connecting the beams on which the warp is wound, legs so that the weaver sits in a European manner, and a framework above the plane of the warp to support the heddles and beater, so that it is a substantial piece of furniture. Andean treadle looms are often made of relatively unfinished pieces of wood, but they still take up more space than a four-stake loom. The beams on which the warp is wound are larger and are able to be rotated, in order to accommodate a very long warp, which can later be cut up. There is a minimum of two shafts, each consisting of two bars between which the heddles are tied, through which the warp yarns pass, and each shaft is connected to a foot treadle. The two shafts are connected to each other over a pulley above, so that when one shaft is lowered by pressing on the treadle, the other shaft is lifted.

It is much faster to weave on a treadle loom. The warp yarns are separated merely by pressing on a treadle with the foot, versus punching down and scraping the warp and inserting the sword. The beating is done by simply bringing the beater forward with one jerk of the hand, in contrast to the short strokes across the sword used on the four-stake loom. Obviously Andean people have felt that it is worth taking the extra time to produce a textile that is not only functional but also beautiful.

Notes

1. The process of learning to weave in Chinchero, another Cuzco-area community, has been eloquently described by Franquemont and Franquemont 1988.
2. The properties of alpaca hair as opposed to sheep's wool are discussed in Switzer 1994, Quiggle 2000.
3. Webster 1972a, p. 108.
4. See for example Bird 1969; E. Franquemont 1986.
5. Müller and Müller 1986, p. 224.
6. For *paña* versus *lloq'e*, see Wilcox 1999, pp. 98–99, 113, 241; Müller and Müller 1986, pp. 39–40. For *lloq'e* yarns, see Goodell 1969, p. 7.
7. Webster 1972a, p. 106.
8. This description of Q'ero spinning is based on Cohen 1980. The film also shows a man plying left-handed, which is probably unusual. For a more detailed description of Cuzco-area spinning, see Franquemont 1985, 1986. The Cohen film, however, does not clearly show the full process that Franquemont describes.
9. Lists of dye plants are provided by Núñez del Prado 1968, p. 247; Webster 1972a, p. 114, as well as by John Cohen. Identifications are available in various sources, of which Soukup 1971 is the most exhaustive. Antúnez de Mayolo 1989 summarizes the literature on Peruvian dye plants.
10. Núñez del Prado (1968, p. 247) also mentions *luma-ch'illka* for deep black. John Cohen (1956 field notes) collected the names *achankaro* for pink, *yana ruku* for black, *punki* (or *tunki*) for yellow, and *pulu* (or *tulu*) for green, a plant also used as a mordant. Soukup (1971, pp. 41, 288) identifies *achanccarai* or *achancaray* as *Begonia* sp. or *Ranunculus krapfia*. He identifies *pullu-pullu* as *Erigeron hieracioides* (p. 125). These plants have not previously been identified as dye plants, however, and positive identification would require further investigation of these plants in Q'ero.
11. Franquemont, Franquemont, and Isbell 1992.
12. More detailed descriptions of similar looms can be found in Rowe 1975 and Zorn 1979.
13. Silverman-Proust 1988b, p. 38; 1998, p. 56.
14. For a general discussion of these weaves, see Rowe 1977a, chapters 10–11.
15. See Rowe 1977a, pp. 82–83.
16. It is, however, also used on Taquile Island (Zorn 1979, p. 216; Martinez and van der Hoeven 1993). Zorn states that the stick is included during warping and compensates for increased take-up.
17. A loom in the American Museum of Natural History collection (41.0/2285).
18. For example, see Rowe 1977b, fig. 7.
19. For example, such a change has occurred earlier in the twentieth century in the Pisac area. See also Silverman 1999, p. 808.
20. The American Museum of Natural History in New York has a loom from Q'ero for a shawl panel that is set up for weaving supplementary-warp patterning in this fashion (40.1/2285). The technique is the same as elsewhere in the Cuzco area.
21. Rowe 1977a, pp. 20–22.
22. Cohen 1980.
23. Silverman 1998, p. 54.
24. This edge binding is similar to that in Rowe 1977a, p. 53, fig. 55, but has additional yarns in the center and at the sides.
25. Flores *et al.* (eds.) (1984, foto 8) shows a man weaving a narrow band of uncertain pattern and function; Müller and Müller (1986, p. 225) is a much clearer photo of the same loom, showing three heddles. Sekino (1984, p. 96 lower left) shows a man weaving a skirt border with four heddles. Silverman (1998, p. 55, fig. 2.4) shows a woman weaving a skirt border with two heddles.
26. See Cahlander with Zorn and Rowe 1980; Zorn 1981; Noble 1982. It is Elayne Zorn who managed to learn to make the fancy sling braids, a task made more difficult by the fact that since it was men's work, the men were reluctant to teach her.
27. Shown in Cohen 1980; see also Goodell 1969, p. 6; Zorn 1981, pp. 48–49.
28. Silverman (1998, p. 69, fig. 2.13) shows a Q'ero man braiding.
29. See LeCount 1990; Callañaupa and Rowe 2001.
30. Webster 1972a, p. 36.

Chapter Four
Textile Design and Aesthetics

Fig. 4.1 Festival coca bag, with *ch'unchu* design, collected in 1955, but probably made *c*. 1900. The brown stripes are probably vicuña hair and have spin stripes. The pattern is in three-color complementary-warp weave. 28 x 16 cm (11 x 6¼ in), including fringe, excluding strap. Strap: 1.42 m x 7 mm (4 ft 7¾ in x ¼ in). The Textile Museum 1974.16.18, gift of Junius B. Bird, Marion Stirling, Mary Frances Recher, and the Peruvian Research Fund.

The designs used in Q'ero woven textiles are comparatively few, but can be elaborated in a variety of ways. In addition, they have evolved and changed over time. During the past century the width of the design bands has increased, with a corresponding reduction in the size of the plain striped areas. The wider stripes allow for more elaborate diamond designs but the human figure (*ch'unchu*) design has been reduced so that the headdress is now the only reference.

Ch'unchu

The oldest surviving Q'ero textiles have a design of a human figure wearing a tall feather headdress (figs. 3.5, 4.1). This design is called *ch'unchu*, a derogatory name for tropical forest Indians, who are accounted inferior and uncivilized by highlanders.[1] The design is used not only in Q'ero but in some other Cuzco-area communities as well, including Pitumarka and the Lares area (fig. 1.8).[2]

The *ch'unchu* is also represented in the dances that are held before, during, and after the pilgrimage to Qoylluriti (see Chapter 5), which takes place at the time of Corpus Christi, not only from Q'ero but also from other attending communities. There are also *ch'unchu* dancers at *Inti Raymi*, a modern imitation Inca festival held in Cuzco a few days after Corpus Christi. The term *chuncho* occurs in early Spanish sources to refer to the indigenous people of the tropical forest in eastern Peru, but the practice of highlanders performing *ch'unchu* dances also goes back to the colonial period in the Cuzco area. There is a document mentioning such dances as early as 1615 and *ch'unchu* dancers are among the designs represented on the later style of colonial wooden cups.[3]

The *ch'unchu* dance probably has a Spanish component since dancers representing savages were included in Corpus Christi celebrations in Spain to symbolize the triumph of Catholic doctrine over non-believers of various kinds.[4] Moreover, feather headdresses similar to those worn by *ch'unchu* dancers were used in early modern Europe in both religious and secular contexts to represent

Fig. 4.2 Detail of a
shawl with *ch'unchu*
design with a tall
headdress, in three-
color complementary-
warp weave. Width of
ch'unchu-design band:
7 cm (2¾ in). American
Museum of Natural
History, New York,
Division of Anthropology
40.1/2201.

Fig. 4.3 Detail of a
shawl with *ch'unchu*
design of two opposing
heads, with all
synthetic dyes, in three-
color complementary-
warp weave. Width of
ch'unchu-design band:
4 cm (1½ in). The Textile
Museum 1974.16.118,
gift of Junius Bird,
Marion Stirling, Mary
Frances Recher, and the
Peruvian Research Fund.

Fig. 4.4 Detail of a shawl with a *ch'unchu* design of opposing headdresses with an *inti* in the center, in three-color complementary-warp weave. Width of *ch'unchu*-design band: 10 cm (4 in). The Textile Museum 1999.7.5, gift of John Cohen.

Fig. 4.5 Poncho with *ch'unchu* **design in three-color complementary-warp weave and warp-resist dyed designs. Overall: 1.52 x 1 m (5 ft x 3 ft 3½ in), including fringe. The Textile Museum 1991.4.1, gift of Mary M. Hill.**

all indigenous inhabitants of the Americas.[5] This tradition overlies the use of feather headdresses (typically using feathers from tropical forest birds) for prestige, religious, and festival purposes throughout pre-Hispanic Peru. A Spanish connection is also suggested by the fact that *ch'unchu* dances are performed in other scattered areas of the former Spanish empire.[6]

The possibility of Spanish influence on or even origin of the *ch'unchu* dance does not mean that the concept has not been

thoroughly integrated into contemporary indigenous belief, however. Some indigenous people identify the *ch'unchu* with the legendary *ñawpa machu*, or old ones, who fled from the highlands into the jungle when the sun rose for the first time.[7] When asked why they danced the *ch'unchu* for Qoylluriti, one Q'ero man told a story about how the *ch'unchu* hid God from the Devil under the feather headdress. The dances performed at Corpus Christi seem to be ironic commentaries on the historical

relationships with other ethnic groups.

These oldest surviving textiles include some shawls that appear to be dyed with natural dyes, and may thus date to the late nineteenth century (figs. 2.2, 3.5), and others dyed with synthetic dyes. The motif is also found on festival coca bags that employ synthetic dyes but may also include some vicuña-hair stripes. One such bag (fig. 4.1) was collected by Oscar Núñez del Prado from a man who had received it from his mother when he was fifteen to eighteen years old, about the time that the railroad to

Fig. 4.6 Detail of a shawl with *ch'unchu* design in three-color complementary-warp weave. The black plain stripes have been folded under in this photograph. Width of the two central design bands: 10.5 cm (4⅛ in). American Museum of Natural History, New York, Division of Anthropology 40.1/2193.

familiar. What is striking is that all of the available preserved textiles that appear to have been dyed only with natural dyes have this *ch'unchu* design as the principal motif.[9] Unfortunately, it is impossible to know whether textiles with this design were preserved because they were more valued or because the *ch'unchu* was the only design used at that time.

The design is definitely a figure against a background, and not the kind of allover pattern found in other Q'ero textile designs. Sometimes the field contains images of birds, small animals, or small rayed diamonds (the *inti*, or sun motif), above the shoulders of the *ch'unchu*. Below the figure's body there may be other iconographic elements, sometimes a design like a plus sign (+), sometimes a V-like form. On one old shawl in the American Museum collection, there is a clear assignment of the "+" and the "V" to separate panels of the piece, except for a single "V" figure on the otherwise all "+" panel (fig. 4.6). The Q'ero often include some interruption in their patterning system, changing one or more motifs, which undoes a sense of absolute consistency (fig. 4.5, *etc.*).

In some examples, presumably dating from a little later, the headdress is of exaggerated size and the body is correspondingly reduced (fig. 4.2). Other variations include a color change through the center of the stripe (fig. 4.6) or a stripe with two figures side-by-side (AMNH 40.1/2198).

Another early type of *ch'unchu* design uses only the head and headdress of the figure, with pairs of them oriented chin-to-chin (fig. 4.3).[10] This design presumably developed out of the full-figure *ch'unchu*.

Cuzco was built, in 1910. It was not new at that time. The only poncho with this design in the current sample is that in fig. 4.5, which is also dyed with synthetic dyes. Regrettably, its collection date is unknown. This version of the design was no longer being woven by the 1950s, when the community was first visited by textile-collecting outsiders. John Cohen found, however, that even in 1989 it was still recognized by young weavers.[8] It appears that there are still enough old textiles in the community for this design to be

Fig. 4.7 Studio photograph of a Q'ero man playing a flute. Photo by Juan Manuel Figueroa Aznar, 1911–24.

Fig. 4.8 Detail of a shawl with *ch'unchu* design of two opposing heads, partly with natural dyes and partly with synthetic dyes. Three-color complementary-warp weave patterning. Loom width: 38 cm (15 in). Collection of Carol Rasmussen Noble.

A poncho with this design, as well as full-figure *ch'unchu* motifs, appears in the earliest available photograph of a Q'ero man (fig. 4.7), taken by Juan Manuel Figueroa Aznar (1878-1951) probably between 1911 (the date on the backdrop) and 1924, when Figueroa's Cuzco studio was taken over by Martín Chambi. The photograph was first published in 1925.[11] The painted backdrop and reclining pose makes the photograph appear as if it might have been composed under the influence of the famous Adolf de Meyer photograph

of the dancer Vaslav Nijinsky in his ballet *L'Après-midi d'un faune*, which premiered in 1912.[12] Figueroa did have an avid interest in the theater. He married Ubaldina Yábar Almarzo, a member of the hacienda-owning family, and took many portraits of them. He also served as mayor and assistant prefect of Paucartambo and as regional representative of the province. It is therefore not so strange that a Q'ero man would have posed for him. The same man appears in other similar Figueroa photographs, designed to illustrate "Indian types" for sale to tourists.[13]

Another probably early example of the *ch'unchu* with chin-to-chin heads is a shawl with narrow pattern stripes and wide black stripes, with some of the pattern yarns dyed with what appears to be indigo, but others with synthetic dyes (fig. 4.8). Other examples of this design are dyed with synthetic dyes, but often the patterns are still relatively narrow (fig. 4.3). A few motifs of this form are included in the poncho in fig. 4.5, along with the full-figure examples. A shawl that appears to have been relatively new when John

Fig. 4.9 Shawl with
ch'unchu design of
two opposing heads,
collected in 1956–57
and probably new at
that time. Three-color
complementary-warp
weave patterning.
84 x 74 cm (33 x 29⅛ in).
American Museum of
Natural History, New
York, Division of
Anthropology 40.1/2206.

Fig. 4.10 Poncho collected in the 1940s, with a *ch'unchu* design of opposing headdresses and an *inti* in the center, flanked by stripes with *inti* designs. Three-color complementary-warp weave patterning. 1.56 x 1.03 m (5 ft 1½ in x 3 ft 8½ in), including fringe. The Textile Museum 1981.9.37, gift of Marion Stirling Pugh.

Fig. 4.11 Shawl with a *ch'unchu* design of opposing headdresses and an *inti* in the center, collected in 1984. Three-color complementary-warp weave patterning, and handwoven edge binding. Loom width: 30 cm (11¾ in). The Textile Museum 1999.7.9, gift of John Cohen.

Cohen collected it in 1956–57 seems to represent one of the latest uses of this variation of the design (fig. 4.9). This variation is no longer being woven.

More recent versions of the *ch'unchu* omit the heads, and have only the two headdresses. A small *inti* is usually placed in the center where the two headdresses come together (fig. 4.4, frontispiece, p. 6).[14] This design was already being woven in the 1940s, as indicated by the poncho in fig. 4.10, which was collected about that time, and is still being woven today. In

older examples the *inti* is usually the same color as the feathers of the *ch'unchu* design (see also fig. 4.11), but in newer examples it may be a contrasting color and there may be an extra tier of shorter feathers (figs. 4.4, 2.3). In older examples the triangular spaces to either side of the *ch'unchu* are treated as triangles, similar to the way in which these spaces were treated when faces instead of an *inti* motif occur in the middle, but in newer examples a more elaborate treatment including diamonds may be used (figs. 4.4, 3.17).

Although a single figure usually fills the width of a stripe, stripes two or three motifs wide are sometimes found (fig. 4.11).

These designs are presented in such a manner that there is no background visual field. The leftover space is filled with the zigzag *chili* pattern (see below). This contributes to an overall visually charged field of abstracted energy, rather than a representation of isolated icons. On these shawls the pattern stripes are wider and the black stripes narrower, and on the most recent examples the black stripe is so narrow it barely registers at all (fig. 5.15).

The *ch'unchu* design is always woven in the three-color complementary-warp weave, in white, red (or pink or orange), and dark blue (or green or purple). Usually, the two patterned stripes in each panel of a shawl are woven in a slightly different color combination. So for instance one stripe will be white, pink, and purple, while the other will be white, red, and dark blue. This type of color scheme has been retained throughout the other changes observable over time.

Fig. 4.13 (opposite)
Shawl with *inti* **designs
in both complementary-
warp weave (paired
floats) and with
supplementary-warp
pattern. 77 x 64 cm
(30¼ x 25¼ in). The
Textile Museum
1974.16.87, gift of
Junius B. Bird, Marion
Stirling, Mary Frances
Recher, and the Peruvian
Research Fund.**

**Fig. 4.14 Shawl
woven by Nicolasa
Quispe Chura.** *Inti*
**designs in three-color
complementary-warp
weave with single
floats. 86 x 62 cm
(33⅞ x 24½ in). The
Textile Museum
1999.7.2, gift of
John Cohen.**

Inti

Another major motif found in Q'ero textiles is a rayed diamond representing *inti*, the sun. This design appears in bands flanking the full-figure *ch'unchu* designs in the oldest surviving shawls. A comparatively early example where the *inti* is a principal design band is the shawl in fig. 4.12, although this piece, like later examples with the *inti* design, is dyed with synthetic dyes. This example is woven with three-color complementary-warp weave, but others are woven with supplementary-warp patterning (fig. 2.4), while others include stripes in both techniques (fig. 4.13). The supplementary-warp patterned *inti* designs usually have a filling of small triangles or diamonds, arranged so that the pattern looks the same on both faces of the fabric.

The narrow examples usually have the center filled with a smaller *inti* or concentric diamonds. The position of the white and colored rays changes from one motif to the next, and from front to back of the same motif. In more recent

examples woven in three colors, a number
of variations are used. A wider style of
filler band may be used (fig. 4.14). The
whole motif may be divided in half
vertically (fig. 4.14, center stripes, 3.20),
or it may be divided by two diagonals into
quarters, or divided into nine or more
(figs. 4.15, 4.16). At times, these smaller
diamonds may be divided in half vertically.
Sometimes small diamonds appear in the
rayed areas of the rectangle (fig. 4.17).
There seems to be less variation among
the examples with supplementary-warp

Fig. 4.17 Shawl with *inti* design, collected in 1957. Side stripes in three-color complementary-warp weave (single floats) and center stripes with supplementary warp. 73 x 68 cm (28¾ x 26¾ in). American Museum of Natural History, New York, Division of Anthropology 40.1/2203.

Fig. 4.18 Girl peeling potatoes, Qolpa K'uchu. Her shawl has *inti* designs in supplementary-warp patterning. Photo by John Cohen, 1956.

Fig. 4.19 Detail of a shawl with *ch'unchu* and *qocha* designs, collected in 1957. Three-color complementary-warp patterning. Width of patterned area: 12 cm (4¾ in). American Museum of Natural History, New York, Division of Anthropology 40.1/2202.

pattern, but occasionally more elaborate designs are found (figs. 4.17, 4.18).

An *inti* made up of fine lines (woven with single floats) may be described by its resemblance to *ichu* grass (*ichu inti*). *Ichu* is a tough grass used for thatch and eaten by llamas, but not alpacas. An *inti* made of wider wiggly lines (woven with floats in alternate pairs) may be compared to a shrub (*tara inti*). An *inti* of contrasting red and white triangles and rectilinear lines in a geometric manner may be called *chili* for its resemblance to the *chili* pattern (see below). An *inti* divided in half vertically may be named *inti chusa*, for its resemblance to the sun as it goes behind a mountain. An *inti* so divided also evokes sun and shadow. A further variant is smaller diamonds appearing in the field of radiating lines, like stars. These terms were collected from several different weavers, but not all weavers would give an identical answer.

Qocha and *chili*

Another common diamond design, woven in three-color complementary-warp weave, is made up of symmetrically arranged zigzags, each composed of lines of triangles (figs. 4.19–4.21). Usually the two zigzags are in contrasting colors, or at least the white and colored yarns exchange position in each half. John Cohen and Steven Webster recorded the name *qocha* (lake) for this design, while Oscar Núñez del Prado recorded *puytu* (rhomboid). If a single such zigzag is

Fig. 4.20 (opposite)
Detail of a shawl with *qocha* design, new in 1974. Three-color complementary-warp weave patterning. Loom width: 31 cm (12¼ in). The Textile Museum 1974.16.98, gift of Junius B. Bird, Marion Stirling, Mary Frances Recher, and the Peruvian Research Fund.

Fig. 4.21 Detail of a poncho with *qocha* design in three-color complementary-warp weave with color alternation like *inti* (paired floats), and supplementary-warp *chili* pattern. Width of *qocha*-design band: 6–6.5 cm (2⅜–2¼ in). American Museum of Natural History, New York, Division of Anthropology 40.1/2215.

woven unopposed, it is called *chili* (after a plant with a scalloped leaf).[15] Fragments of this motif are also often used as a filler on the edges of the *ch'unchu* headdress plus *inti* design.

The earliest available example of the *qocha* design occurs in a shawl that also has full-figure *ch'unchu* designs, dyed with synthetic dyes (fig. 4.19). Here it is woven with more threads (floats) per triangle than is typical in later examples. The poncho in Martín Chambi's 1934 photograph (fig. 5.7) has the *qocha* design

Fig. 4.22 Festival coca bag with *chili* design in supplementary warp and *ch'unchu* design in three-color complementary-warp weave, collected 1957. The brown stripes may be vicuña hair and have spin stripes. 23 x 16 cm (9 x 6¼ in), including fringe (strap missing). The Textile Museum 1999.7.12, gift of John Cohen.

Fig. 4.23 Detail of a shawl with *qocha* design in supplementary warp, collected in 1973. Loom width: 30 cm (11¾ in). Private collection.

with the same number of floats as is still used for it today (fig. 4.20).

Although usually the *qocha* design is woven with the three-color complementary-warp weave with a simple color alternation like the *ch'unchu*, occasionally it is woven with the same type of color alternation as the *inti* design (fig 4.21).

Both *qocha* and *chili* are also sometimes woven with supplementary-warp patterning (fig. 4.22). In this case two adjacent triangles are the same color, so together they appear more like diamonds.

Sometimes the diagonal outlines are accented by ground warp (white) floats, alternately on one face of the fabric or the other, again preserving the double-faced effect (fig. 4.23).

Fig. 4.24 Shawl from the Ocongate area with patterns in supplementary warp and embroidery. 51 x 44 cm (20 x 17¼ in), excluding ties. The Textile Museum 1999.7.27, gift of John Cohen.

Ocongate-area designs

The style of the neighboring Ocongate area employs only supplementary-warp patterning for the designs, not complementary-warp weave (fig. 4.24). The designs used are readily distinguishable from those of Q'ero discussed above, and are composed in such a way that more of the supplementary warp appears on one side (which presumably would read as the front) than on the other. Embroidery of a contrasting color that imitates the effect of the supplementary-warp patterning may enliven the effect.

The designs typically consist of diamonds formed by diagonally arranged rows of parallelograms. Sometimes these diamonds are relatively short and wide and lack outlines, while in other cases the diamonds are even-sided and are framed by a linear diamond with another diamond in the center. Sometimes a linear diamond is filled with a related motif known as *t'ika* or flower (see the outer stripes of the poncho in fig. 1.5).

Fig. 4.25 Daily-use
coca bag with
Ocongate-style design
in supplementary
warp, collected in
1976. 52 x 27 cm
(20½ x 10⅝ in). The
Textile Museum
1999.7.16, gift of
John Cohen.

Since about 1975, some Q'ero weavers have been using these designs, particularly in those hamlets that are nearest to the Ocongate-style area, and the use of such designs seems to have been gradually increasing. In central Q'ero these designs seem to occur primarily on textiles of lesser importance, such as daily-use coca bags and carrying cloths (figs. 4.25, 2.11). In these fabrics Q'ero characteristics such as the plain stripe layout or spin stripes may still be present. Ocongate-area designs are also used in garments intended to mask identity such as those that are worn for the *tinkuy* dance after Carnival or by Qolla dancers for the pilgrimage to Qoylluriti who are intended to represent neighboring people (see Chapter 5).[16] On the other hand, in K'allakancha, a hamlet affiliated with Totorani and close to Paucartambo, all the young girls were weaving and wearing these designs, including on their shawls, by 1985.[17]

Flanking stripes

The principal pattern stripes on shawls and festival bags, and sometimes on daily-use coca bags and ponchos, are normally flanked by narrow three-color complementary-warp weave stripes in a contrasting set of colors, often yellow, green, and red. Designs include alternating triangles, diamonds, S-motifs, and small *inti* motifs.

All these small elements, described separately, constitute the parameters of the Q'ero aesthetic.[18]

Aesthetic Observations
John Cohen

The Q'ero tradition is old, and the weavers of each generation restate their cultural inheritance in the patterns they weave. For them, learning their traditions is a matter of practicing life as they live it. There is no organized system or school to categorize or give instruction in their body of knowledge.

Each visitor to Q'ero, however, necessarily constructs a terminology to describe the Q'ero phenomena in terms consistent with his or her own world view. Anthropologist, textile researcher, ethnomusicologist, photographer, filmmaker, mestizo guide, visiting priest, salesman, or missionary: all answer to their own vision and vocabulary, and translate what they observe, using the inadequate descriptive systems available.

In 1956 my framework for looking at Andean textiles was shaped by my training in the visual arts, and specifically in my study with Josef Albers at Yale University. Albers had been a teacher at the Bauhaus in Germany, and later a seminal artistic force at Black Mountain College in North Carolina before he came to the Yale Art School. He transmitted the viewpoint of the modern artist, yet his own training had been in the craft tradition. He often stated his deep appreciation of American Indian art, and particularly his admiration for Inca architectural works. His wife Anni Albers, a world-renowned weaver, dedicated her 1965 book *On Weaving*, "To my great teachers, the weavers of ancient Peru."

Josef Albers often quoted the gestalt psychologists whose theoretical work was concerned with a scientific understanding of visual perception. In this way, the vocabulary of gestalt psychologists affected my descriptions of Andean textiles. Certain gestalt principles were illuminated in the ethnographic weaving of the Andes as well as in pre-Columbian fabrics.

Fig. 4.26 Shawl with modern *ch'unchu* design, collected in 1989. Three-color complementary-warp patterning. 71 x 62 cm (28 x 24½ in). The Textile Museum 1999.7.5, gift of John Cohen.

Figure-ground

This term refers to a visual relationship where the background and the figure are of equal importance. Neither is in front; each determines the other; there is no foreground or background. Frequently referred to as an "interlocking" pattern, this effect is manifested in shapes such as the meander.

The Q'ero also use figure-ground in a linear system, for example in the color patterned stripes where both sides of the fabric contain the same design, with the colors reversed. In modern Q'ero textiles, the figure-ground relationship takes on another aspect where three distinct images share their boundaries so that the *ch'unchu*, *inti*, and *chili* patterns define each other (fig. 4.26).

In the oldest Q'ero shawls, the *ch'unchu* figures are shown clearly in front of a background. As the form of the weaving evolved and changed during the course of the twentieth century, the integrated figure-ground relationship became more evident, to the point where the figures have become subsidiary to the predominant patterning.

Interrupted pattern

This effect occurs when a regular repeated pattern covers an entire visual field, but one single element is differentiated by change of color, shape, or placement in a sequence, causing it to stand out visually, thereby interrupting the regularity of the overall pattern. This can be a very simple effect, or extremely complex as in the case of Paracas mantles, which contain color sequences as well as orientation sequences. Andean weavers today take delight in introducing visual interruptions to the traditional patterns they make (fig. 4.24).

In Q'ero shawls, the placement of yellow design elements in the borders of the main patterned stripes introduces a counter rhythm to that in the main patterned stripes (fig. 4.26).

Configuration

This phenomenon concerns the way the human mind/eye organizes groupings or figures within a larger field of elements. An example is the way the eye sees constellations or groupings within the thousands of stars in the sky. It has to do with seeking order, or with structuring visual elements into recognizable patterns. The placement or sequence of stripes on an Andean textile is a direct example of this phenomenon put into practice.

On recent Q'ero fabrics, an extremely complex aspect of this configuration phenomenon is achieved (fig. 4.26). On viewing this group of interacting *inti–ch'unchu–chili* patterns, the mind's eye finds itself either reading the separate images, or seeing them as part of a larger hexagonal form. This phenomenon is also experienced with shawls and ponchos where the patterned stripes are so wide, with so little space between them, that visual elements from one figure are configured with elements from an adjacent design (fig. 5.15).

Returning to Paracas mantles, there are several levels of visual configuration at work. The initial appearance of an entire mantle will resemble a checkerboard. Further examination will reveal that its pattern is organized along diagonals. A third reading, along a horizontal axis, reveals that the pattern may be viewed as a series of repeated color sequences.[19]

Gestalt psychology deals not only with single, discreet visual phenomena. It introduces the concept that the configuration of a total entity or individual has a distinct, recognizable gestalt (or total impression). The gestalt of a Rembrandt drawing is different from that of a Mondrian. The Rembrandt is made up of a great variety of searching and often incomplete gestural lines, while the Mondrian has clean, crisp, decisive, straight lines and completed elements (squares and rectangles). The Mondrian has a "good" gestalt compared to the indistinct gestalt of the Rembrandt.

Another way of demonstrating how gestalt works is in its aspect of correspondence between different forms. For example, take the syllabic words *takititi* and *maluma*, and connect them with either of these visual images, a curvy, soft, S-shaped amoeba form or a pointy, splintered, angular "zigzag," and the correct connection becomes evident.

Q'ero weavers have given their descriptions of variations of *inti*, which can be a matter of their naming the correspondence between the basic sun image (a diamond shape with diagonal lines radiating out from it) and the nature of its visual/verbal counterpart. The *inti* is seen as being like *ichu* grass, the *tara* shrub, the sun behind the mountain, or a geometric pattern called *chili*. This use of compared images is a form of interpretation used by the Q'ero to describe shared similarities between things, just as the gestalt system demonstrates. This occurs in a visual/verbal setting and does not affect the significance or symbolism of meaning in these objects.

Christine Franquemont reports how Quechua speakers in Chinchero, another Cuzco-area community, compare an agricultural field to the broad, unpatterned plain-weave areas of a shawl, referring to it as *pampa*. (The same term is used in Q'ero.) In another case where the woven patterns (*pallay*) are like harvested potatoes, she adds, "This does not mean that the woven *pallay* is a symbol of, or stands for the potato harvest. Instead both are ordered cultural processes that delineate a field."[20] She discusses the abstract nature of the pattern names as implying a logic of associations rather than representation. A similar pattern of thought seems to underlie the names of the *inti* variations in Q'ero.

In my own early 1957 encounter with these variations of the *inti*, I realized they could be accounted for in terms of a menu of styles. *Ichu inti* was a linear style, whereas *inti pili* consisted more of small geometric forms. This distinction was made by several (female) weavers. I also tested this vocabulary on some of the men wearing these patterns. They laughed. It also appears that *pili* (not in the dictionaries consulted) may refer specifically to patterns made with supplementary warp rather than complementary warp.

Considering the types of images used not only in the textiles but also in the Q'ero songs, it is clear that they are all real elements in Q'ero life, and many of them probably have some symbolic power as well. Just the fact that they have been woven, sung, and danced to gives them a special attention. We can enumerate, interpret, and approach their meanings, but not attain them. Ultimately their significance to the Q'ero is inaccessible. But even if these iconographic messages remain indecipherable to us, they are still worthy of our consideration.

Music and weaving

A man passes high on the hill above, playing his flute. People in the valley recognize him by the way he plays the melody. An old woman in Q'ero looks at a finely woven fabric and identifies the weaver who made it by the way in which it was woven.

Although the Q'ero play a variety of musical instruments, including transverse flutes, panpipes, and vertical flutes made of plastic, only one of these, the *pinkulu*, is used for the distinctive four-note tunes that are heard only in Q'ero (fig. 5.14). These emblematic songs are built around only a few notes and utilize a limited range of subjects: *phalcha* flowers, *wallata* birds, *serena* (waterfalls), and *turpa* flowers. Similarly, Q'ero textiles use a comparatively limited number of design motifs: *inti*, *ch'unchu*, *qocha*, and *chili*. Yet the visual effect is full of variations.

In the traditional weaving there is a definite ordering of the sequence of stripes that run from the edge of the fabric to the patterned areas. Another rhythm of patterning is used lengthwise in the textile. Most obviously it is seen in the *inti* or *ch'unchu* patterns that alternate within regular visual blocks or frames within the stripes. These blocks are roughly the same size (5–10 cm or 2–4 in on older fabrics, bigger on recent ones). But the smaller patterns in the flanking stripes have a different kind of color repeat, where the color combination will be the same for three motifs before changing, or two colors might alternate (figs. 4.20, 4.26).

Musically this would be described as two separate beats playing at the same time (for example waltz, 3/4 time, and polka, 2/4). The Q'ero do not play waltzes or polkas, but if you ask three Q'ero men to play the "*Wallata*" flute tune, they will comply but will play in three different keys, each at their own starting and finishing point. Musicologists call this practice "heterophony," and it can be seen as a form of music that permits the maximum expression of an individual while adhering to strict traditional practice and extreme limits.

From a slight viewing distance, the yellow figures on the shawl in fig. 4.26 stand out because of their greater light reflectance and brightness. But the rhythm of the yellow figures is often unrelated to that of the larger patterns adjacent to them. Visually this sets up a strange pulsing sensation, and on a new shawl where the main pattern dominates, it creates a complex overall effect that pulsates across the entire visual field. This overall combination of differing, independent rhythms existing in the same field, is heard in the most concentrated aspects of the Q'ero Carnival music, where everyone is playing and singing in a different time, key, and rhythm (see Chapter 5).

Notes

1. For a Q'ero myth about their tropical forest neighbors, see Yábar 1923.
2. Examples from Pitumarka and vicinity and from Huancarani are illustrated in Silverman and Chauca 1993; see Seibold 1992, pp. 183–84 for a Lares-area example.
3. Dean 1999, p. 255, note 13, mentions the document. Wilson 1991, p. 209, mentions the cup motifs.
4. Dean 1999, p. 12. She also cites an early seventeenth-century drawing of Guaman Poma (her fig. 7, p. 57, his fol. 783) that shows sons of indigenous caciques dressed in European masquerade costumes, she says representing Muslims, dancing with staves before an altar with the Eucharist. Guaman Poma's drawing of a purported tropical forest dance (fol. 322, Wilson 1991's fig. 5) does not resemble modern *ch'unchu* dancing except possibly for the headdress of one figure.
5. Wilson 1991, p. 209.
6. Sallnow (1987, p. 222) mentions places in the dept. of Puno, Peru, and a town in northern Chile; Wilson (1991, p. 219, note 24) mentions Tarija, Bolivia.
7. Müller and Müller 1986, p. 136. See also Gow 1974, pp. 72–73; his data is from Pinchimuro in the Ocongate-style area.
8. Silverman (1998, p. 150, and elsewhere) says that the Q'ero call this version of the design *ñawpa ch'unchu* (*ch'unchu* of the past).
9. Additional examples include TM1999.7.8, AMNH 40.1/2200, and Meisch (ed.) 1997, cat. no. 200, pp. 124–25 (all shawls). The shawl in fig. 3.5 has previously been illustrated in Wilson 1991, p. 229, figs. 2–3 (the accession number given incorrectly in the captions).
10. Silverman (1998, p. 148, and elsewhere) says that the Q'ero call this version of the design *ch'unchu simicha* (*ch'unchu* with a small mouth).
11. Ranney 2000, p. 120, note 56. Benavente 1995 is another important source on Figueroa.
12. This photograph has been frequently reproduced but see for example, Nectoux (ed.) 1989, p. 93.
13. Poole 1997, p. 188, fig. 7.6. In this photograph, the poncho is not visible, but the rest of his clothes are clearly the same, including a black tunic. Poole's book has a chapter on Figueroa and she also illustrates some of his self-portraits and Yábar family portraits.
14. Silverman (1998, p. 148–49 and elsewhere) says that the Q'ero call this version of the design, *ch'unchu inti pupu* (*ch'unchu* sun navel).
15. This interpretation is from C. Franquemont 1986, p. 332. Silverman (1994, p. 76 and 1998, p. 66) cites three other definitions.
16. For a Qolla dancer, see Silverman-Proust 1989, photo p. 20, taken in 1980.
17. Silverman-Proust 1988a, pp. 238–39. Additional illustrations in Sekino 1984, pp. 31, 49 top, 69, 76 lower right.
18. Webster (1972a, note 22, p. 352) reports being told that different textile motifs referred to former caste or class distinctions, the existence of which he thought unlikely in such a small community. On further query he indicated that this information was from Eduardo De Bary (of the hacienda Ccapana), who said that *inti* motifs represented the highest caste and *qocha* the lowest. The fact that this was not a story he heard in Q'ero reinforces Webster's observations of the lack of such a system.
19. See Paul 1992.
20. C. Franquemont 1986, p. 331.

Chapter Five
Religion and Festivals

The Q'eros consider themselves Catholics, but a priest seldom visits. Their religious practice incorporates some indigenous beliefs and rituals, particularly for the fertility of their lands and animals, as well as for their own well-being. The natural world is sacred, and is personified in Pachamama, or Mother Earth, the *apus* or mountain peaks, *awkis* or smaller hills, and *khuyas* or stone amulets representing herd animals. Offerings are made to these spirits by various means.

Ordinary people make these offerings on appropriate occasions, but some people are considered to have special powers, for example if they survive a lightning strike. Such people then seek specialized training in ritual practice. They are called *paqo*, often translated as "shaman," although "ritual specialist" might be more accurate.[1] They are usually men, only occasionally women. They can perform divinations and understand more readily a problem and carry out a more effective ritual solution. A small number of *paqos* are feared for their presumed malevolence, however, while at least a few Q'eros do not believe

in the powers of *paqos* at all. The Q'eros' tenacious grip on the old ways marks them as different and powerful to other Andean communities. Reportedly, *paqos* from other parts of the Cuzco area go to Q'ero to receive initiation rites.[2]

Like all their Andean neighbors, the Q'eros perform the coca blow (*k'intu*) ritual. They arrange coca leaves in groups of three, hold them in front of their lips and blow across them, while thinking of the most powerful local *apu*, before they ingest the leaves. The Q'eros are also very serious about divining and reading coca leaves, which for them can tell both fortune and the future. It is all part of the continual act of placating the spirits that reside in the mountains.

A burned offering, usually called *despacho* (a Spanish word) in the Cuzco area, is made as a communication or message to the spirits whenever needful (fig. 5.2). Such an offering can be a family affair, such as to begin the herd fertility rituals, or a private communication by an individual, or be performed by a *paqo* on behalf of a client as a means of solving a

particular problem. The ritual is begun by laying out a large number of small packets of cloth, paper, or plastic, containing coca, the *khuya*, and other small objects such as strings, powders, stones, and seeds, as well as such exotic items as camelid fetuses or starfish. These objects are all laid out on a ground cloth, often a produce bag, which serves as a table or *mesa*, and designates a zone of spiritual/religious importance. Coca is always the main burned offering but *tarwi*, *kañiwa*, or amaranth, animal fat, flowers, sugar and other purchased foods, incense, and so on, are also used, depending on the purpose of the offering. The ritual includes coca chewing, drinking and libations, prayers, and, in the case of the herd rituals, music. During a *despacho* Cohen witnessed, the man officiating took two pieces of yarn, a red one and a white one, and joined them. Indicating that these were the colors of the Peruvian flag, he said, "With these Peruvian threads, we tie the world together."

While it is beyond the scope of this book to detail all the various rituals the Q'ero observe, we here provide descriptions of those that are textile related in some way.[3] Steven Webster reports that Carnival and Easter are distinguished from the Corpus Christi festival by being referred to as *p'achawan*, that is, with [new] clothing (*p'acha*), and for which people are most lavishly dressed (see the description under "Carnival", below).[4] We describe Corpus Christi because of its association with *ch'unchu* dancers, an important textile motif, and the camelid fertility rituals because these animals are the main source of fiber.

Easter and the Blessing of the Textiles

During fieldwork in 1969–70, Steven Webster and his wife Lois recorded a ceremony in which the finest textiles woven during the preceding year, mostly women's shawls and men's scarves, were blessed as part of the Easter celebration (figs. 5.3–5.6). The Easter festival (*Paskwa puxllay*) extends from Saturday evening through the Wednesday after Easter, during which a number of feasts are given, together with music and dancing. On Easter Sunday, two crosses and two

Fig. 5.4 Ritual meal of
the elders at Easter,
on a terrace below the
chapel. Photo by Steven
Webster, 1970.

banners (referred to as *tataycha–mamaycha*, or *tatanchis–mamanchis*, "our [little] father–mother") kept in the church are carried first to an old deserted roofless chapel above the village and then back to the church, in the course of which they are paraded under an arch hung with the textiles. A band consisting of two flutes and two drums (called *chirimoya*) marches around the village serenading the feasts and preceding the parading of the standards.

The day begins with a general feast soon after sunrise in the church plaza. The format of such a feast is as follows (see fig. 5.4, which shows the second feast). A small central table is set up, with a line of produce sacks extending as far as twelve meters (forty feet) on either side. The mayor and chief officials sit at the table, flanked by other male elders, seated in rank order. The feast sponsors (hosts) and musicians are saluted by blowing on conch-shell trumpets, followed by general cheers. Male assistants to the sponsor serve the food and drink at a run, back and forth from the houses where it is being prepared. The older women and younger men stand on the peripheries, while the younger women do the cooking. Everyone gets to eat, however.

The maize beer is served in wooden cups (*q'ero*) in a ritual format. The sponsors stand in front of the officials and elders and call out "*Kayta!*" ("Here!"). Their assistants bring two or three pairs of cups with beer and the sponsors then hand each pair to certain individual guests. Then the guest hands one of the pair on to another guest, who responds with thanks, and both drink rapidly without removing the cup from their lips. Cheering follows. The guest who received a cup from another guest always hands it back to the person from whom he had received it, and this person then returns both to the servers by tossing them into the server's outstretched poncho. The server then runs off to refill the cups. All of the older men seated at the feast receive maize beer in this way.

At about mid-morning, twenty to thirty men and women in dress clothing begin to dance in a circle in the church plaza, then break away to lead the musicians and take the crosses and banners up the hillside toward the old chapel (fig. 5.3). The dancers take a circuitous path, frequently doubling back on themselves. At the chapel there is more dancing and then the dancers kneel while a ritual advisor takes the crosses and banners inside the chapel and intones a long chant. He shields them from the sun with a blanket since the chapel is roofless. He and a boy remain to guard them while the festivities continue below. Children with branches sweep the church plaza and the trails through the village. People not involved in these proceedings watch eagerly from the hillside above.

At the church doorway, the men prepare a framework (*arko*, or arch) of three timbers on which the textiles will be draped. The poles themselves are wrapped in black *bayeta* and ropes are made ready on the crossbar. About forty to fifty elders and officials then make their way up to a terrace below the chapel where a table and cloth has been laid for the next feast, and the food (potatoes and meat) and beer

**Fig. 5.5 Raised arch
with the textiles on it,
Easter. Photo by Steven
Webster, 1970.**

are served (fig. 5.4). During the drinking,
the ritual advisor gives a long prayer
blessing the feast and makes an offering
of beer on each corner of the little table
and on the ground with each of the two
cups of beer. Then all the food is divided
up and carried off in their ponchos by
the men for their families. After an
interruption of rain, six to eight rounds
of bread (supplied by a merchant) are
reverently produced, divided among the
participants and eaten.

Then a group of officials go to the old
chapel to form a procession with the
banners and crosses, to bring them back
down to the church. Meanwhile, with
what seems like exploding excitement,
most people rush back down to the
church to dress the *arko*. The men lay the
shawls and vicuña scarves that have been
brought over the crossbeam and lash them
in place, while the women and children
watch. The presence of both men's and
women's textiles for this ceremony is
probably significant and correlates with
the presence of both men and women in
the procession. A rope strung beneath the

Fig. 5.6 Parading the crosses and banners under the arch to bless the textiles, Easter. Photo by Steven Webster, 1970.

weavings is hung with other items, not all of which could be identified, but appeared to include coca pouches, paraphernalia for other rituals such as the herd ceremonies described below, and dried animals or parts of animals that are also sometimes used in rituals. In a relaxed moment after the *arko* is ready, one participant who is leaving tosses an old rag onto it, remarking that this is his contribution. The gesture is greeted with much laughter and hilarity and a few wags make an effort to tie it in place. This incident reveals both the

Q'eros' disdain of false sanctimony and the real ritual value of their weavings, as well as their sense of humor.

The men each use a long forked pole to lift the *arko* in a great show of force and struggling coordination (fig. 5.5). While the men hold the arch and its textiles aloft, the crosses and banners are marched underneath it on the trail coming downhill, all to the accompaniment of music (fig. 5.6). Then the *arko* is lowered, the textiles unlashed and reclaimed by the women. The women closest to the bundles

call out the names of weavers, apparently identifying them by the appearance of their work, and pass the textiles along to be returned to the owner. Subsequently, there is another feast for the whole community in the church plaza, this time with over sixty elders, and with more eating and fewer interruptions for salutes and blessings.

Fig. 5.7 Q'ero man
wearing a poncho with
the *qocha* design at the
pilgrimage festival of
Qoylluriti. Photograph
by Martín Chambi, 1934.

Qoylluriti

People from Q'ero participate in the
pilgrimage to Qoylluriti (Star Snow) at
the time of Corpus Christi in late May
or early June (fig. 5.7). The shrine of
Qoylluriti is located just below the glacier
of a peak called Qoylluriti by the Q'ero,
at the southeastern end of the Ayakachi
range of glacial peaks. Adjacent peaks
called Sinakara and Qolqepunku (Silver
Portal) also feature in the ceremonies.
All these mountains are considered *apus*.
Although this pilgrimage now has a

Catholic gloss, it has many indigenous
elements.[5] No definite information is
available about pre-Hispanic or early
colonial observances at the site, but many
Andean festivals that took place at this
time of year were subsumed under Corpus
Christi after the Spanish conquest.

The Catholic Church dates the origin
of the pilgrimage to around 1780,
coinciding with a major indigenous
rebellion in the area. The version of the
origin story told to Steven Webster, which
reflects indigenous beliefs, is that the boy

Fig. 5.8 Featherwork *ch'unchu* headdress. Maximum height: 98 cm (38½ in). American Museum of Natural History, New York, Division of Anthropology 40.1/2286 and 2272.

Jesus appeared and played with a shepherd boy. Because of persecution from the local villagers, Jesus withdrew into the massive rock that is now the center of the shrine, leaving his image on the surface. It is not surprising that a rock is the focus of indigenous veneration since rocks are sacred in pre-Hispanic belief. In the mid-twentieth century, the Church touched up the image on the rock and built a concrete building over it with a corrugated iron roof, as part of their attempt to co-opt what had previously been a primarily indigenous ritual. The pilgrimage is made both by indigenous people from a number of surrounding communities and by mestizos, who each have their own observances. Presumably because of the significant efforts in recent decades of the Church to control the pilgrimage, the tendency has been for mestizos and tourists to attend Qoylluriti in increasing numbers, and indigenous people less so.[6] The festival goes on for five days.

Webster reports that two separate groups of people make a pilgrimage from Q'ero Llaqta, leaving in different directions, and taking with them religious objects.[7] One group descends about halfway down to the maize fields to a shrine called Kamara, at about 2600 m (8500 ft) altitude, while a larger group proceeds on a longer trip up over the passes at the northeast end of the Ayakachi range to Qoylluriti. At Kamara, Webster observed a blessing and cleansing of the staffs and conch-shell trumpets of the officials, while another report describes a stone with a vaguely llama-shaped form on one side and the pilgrims saying prayers for the benefit of the llama herds.[8] The pilgrimage groups are

composed mainly of one chosen kin group but represent the community as a whole.

The other group of pilgrims leaves the ritual center for Qoylluriti in the evening and throughout the night traverse one or more of the valleys of Q'ero, being feasted in several houses and supplemented by additional pilgrims on their way to the pass. They take two boxes with sacred objects, one of which is called Señor Qoylluriti (an image of Christ). A band consisting of two flutes and two drums plays throughout the journey. As the pilgrims approach the head of each valley, as they depart the last one, and again just before crossing the final crest of the community domain, where there is a cairn of stones, they pause to play a salute with conch-shell trumpets and cane flutes. At the border, they also pray and dance. Upon arrival at Ancasi, on the other side of the pass, the Q'ero boxes with sacred objects are placed in the local church for prayers and the dancers dance both in honor of entering and of departing. Another stop is made at the chapel in Uskuyuni, where the image is considered to be the consort of the one from Q'ero, and another stop at the entrance to the site of Qoylluriti. The Q'ero pilgrims arrive at Qoylluriti a day later than those from other indigenous communities.

Both the Q'ero groups return to Q'ero in order to arrive at the ritual center at sunrise on the day of Corpus Christi, when a feast is held. While those preparing the feast await them and peer up or down the mountain valley, the returning groups march down from the passes or up from the jungle, dancing and playing music along the trail and stopping at other sacred

Fig. 5.10 Musicians and dancers at the Corpus Christi festival. Photo by Steven Webster, 1970.

sites as on the outward journey. The eating, drinking, dancing, and singing continues for about three days and nights.

Like other groups attending Qoylluriti, the majority of the dancers are men representing *ch'unchus*, or tropical forest Indians, who are considered savages (see also Chapter 4). The *ch'unchu* dancers wear a tall headdress of red macaw feathers, similar to that depicted on the textiles, and carry a staff of chonta wood (figs. 5.8–5.10).[9] They also wear a white shirt, a sash with mirror bangles, and a

cascade of feathers hanging down their back. Strings of shorter blue feathers may be tied on to the arms or as a necklace. During some of the Corpus Christi festivities in Q'ero Llaqta, the feather headdresses and back tassels are carried mounted on staffs rather than worn. Both the feathers and the staffs come from the jungle. An anthropologist who did fieldwork in the 1960s among the Wachipaeri, who are the Q'eros' lowland forest neighbors, reports that indeed the Wachipaeri were trading feathers to the

Q'ero at that time.[10] The music used for these dances is completely distinctive within the Q'ero repertoire but similar music is used for *ch'unchu* dances by other communities who go on this pilgrimage. A transverse six-note flute, *pitu*, is used only for this music, along with drums.[11] The dancers form pairs, clashing their staffs. With skipping steps they form X-shapes, figure eights, and circles. Each sequence is immediately repeated in reverse.

In 1970 and 1977, when Webster attended parts of these ceremonies, the

Q'ero dancers included men dressed as mestizo authorities who carry and crack whips. These dancers wore jackets and knee pants with decorative trim, white stockings and shoes, and upside-down *monteras* (that is, with the red underside upwards) over their *ch'ullus* (fig. 5.10). They also wore a pair of slings with large end tassels. These dancers were not identified to Webster as Qolla dancers, after people from the Lake Titicaca area, as is customary for some other communities in the area, but rather as "*matadores … runa huyuna*" ("matadors … fleeing people"). By 1980, however, there were Qolla dancers from Q'ero who wore shawls in the style of the Ocongate area and who are considered more acculturated.[12] The Qolla are herders of llamas and alpacas and are also familiar as merchants. There are several store owners in Ocongate who are from this area, and in October and November buyers from the south come to Ocongate to buy wool and alpaca hair. They also come to Q'ero to trade meat and *bayeta* for alpaca hair. For this reason, they have an association with mestizo life, and tend often to be danced by mestizos. They generally wear a *montera*, a white knitted mask, a braided sling diagonally across the chest and back, the skin of a baby llama, and an indigenous woman's shawl.

A few young men are dressed in bear costumes (*ukuku*). The costume consists of a narrow fabric with rows of long dark-brown pile, probably llama hair, that hangs down nearly to ankle length in front and back. They wear a knitted mask over their head and speak in a falsetto voice. The tale of the Bear's Son appears to be of Spanish origin, but has become integrated into indigenous folklore in the Andes.[13] Among the incidents in this story is that a half-bear half-man *ukuku* is able to vanquish a damned soul (*kukuchi*). Such damned souls are thought to inhabit the glaciers, where they fruitlessly seek forgiveness from the *apu*, adding to the dangers of cold and chasms that glaciers normally possess. In 1970, the dancers from Q'ero included twelve *ch'unchus*, eight *ukukus*, and four to six matadors.

At Qoylluriti people from all the Q'ero communities always camp in the same place, on the outskirts of the sanctuary grounds, on the northwest or right bank of the stream descending through the pilgrimage site (fig. 5.7). Some observers mention another sacred stone, the Q'ero stone, on the site of the Q'ero camp.[14] Most other groups camp on the opposite bank, where the shrine is situated.

In addition to the rock with the image of Christ, there is another rock nearby, on which has been painted an image of the Virgin, called the Virgin of Fatima (the Fatima grotto), where women go for help with weaving. They weave small fabrics to leave as offerings.[15] People also build miniature houses, corrals, and livestock out of small stones in the hope of securing good health and the fertility of their animals.

On the night before the conclusion of the festival, several men put on their bear costumes. A few hours after dark, a procession is organized of these *ukuku* dancers, from Q'ero and other communities, in 1977 including perhaps forty to fifty men, each carrying a lighted candle. While the valley full of pilgrims watches and groans or cheers and bands play spontaneously, the procession of *ukukus*, points of light in the cold darkness, dramatically climbs a faltering zigzag path up to the face of the glacier hanging down from the mountain, an ascent that takes about an hour. There, each *ukuku* removes a large block of ice and laboriously carries it back down to their encampments to be distributed among their people. Between 1972 and 1978 there were two such processions, one of Paucartambo communities (including Q'ero) and one of Quispicanchis communities, each taking a different route.[16] The ceremony extends into the early morning. The procession is an act of penance. Indigenous people including the Q'eros attribute medicinal properties or purity to glacial ice or snow, and sometimes save some of the water.

The Q'ero do not participate in the procession to Tayankani and Ocongate that completes the pilgrimage for many other indigenous groups, but instead hold their own ceremonies. Late in the day they go to the shrine, some dressed in their dance costumes, to hear a mass and receive the sacraments. A few elders approach the rock and kneel in prayer, then withdraw to begin the dancing. The series of dances, in which the Q'ero alternate with another indigenous group, continues all night.

Fig. 5.11 Standing stone in the corral. Photo by John Cohen, 1989.

Cohen in 1977, "We are used to living between the jungles and the mountains. In these heights we plant potatoes, and from the land we are always able to subsist. We make the land produce, always under commitment to the *awkis*, performing offerings [giving invitations] to the *awkis* and to the land [Pachamama]."

People are grateful to these spirits that inhabit the mountains and the earth, and live their lives in accord with (dependent on) the forces of nature. They also have a deep understanding of the power that nature exerts over them. Their offerings to the *awkis* are made as much out of fear as out of appreciation. In their daily lives the mountain spirits are evoked constantly when the Q'ero take coca leaves, or when they pour offerings of maize beer to the earth before beginning important work. The songs and flute tunes that are heard in the pastures throughout the day are also a form of prayer or commitment to the *awkis*. In the corral, there is an upright standing stone, on which they burn coca leaves to the *awkis* in order to protect the health and fertility of the animals (fig. 5.11).

The most dramatic form of Q'ero commitment to the *awkis* is seen in their festivals that center round the flocks. The two major festivals are the *Axata Uxuchichis* (Let's drink maize beer) and *Phalchay* (after the name of a red flower; the first "h" indicates an aspiration after the "p.") The first of these festivals is held in July or August to celebrate the harvest of the maize and the male llamas who have transported the crop up from the jungle, and it correlates roughly with Santiago (July 25) although this correlation is not as strong as elsewhere in Peru. The second festival, *Phalchay*, is for the health and fertility of the alpacas. The date of this festival is determined by the Christian Carnival celebration, which takes place at a different date each year in either February or March.

Herding rituals

The most important festivals in Q'ero are organized around their domestic animals, the alpacas and llamas. The interdependence of the flocks and the Q'eros is acknowledged in many ways. They make regular offerings to the *awkis* and *apus* to insure the health, strength, and fertility of the animals. Their language is curious in how it expresses this interdependence, for they say they make their offerings under "commitment" to the gods. As Mariano Flores told John

Fig. 5.12 Family group praying to the mountain in the llama ceremony. Photo by Emilio Rodriguez, 1976–77.

The maize and llama ceremony

The date of this ceremony is determined by a series of agricultural factors: the maize crop from the jungle has been harvested and transported to the Q'eros' mountain homes, the early potato crops have been planted, some selected maize kernels have been sprouted by warmth and moisture and are ground up, cooked and allowed to ferment, to make the maize beer that is used in the ceremony.

Different families use different dates for the ceremony, determined by their state of preparedness. Some do their ritual indoors, others in the corral with the animals. On the day of the festival there has been the final preparation of the beer and the ritual spinning and braiding of special yarns that will be used to decorate the animals. Along with drinking and ceremonial coca, there is chanting and singing in the house. In the late afternoon, an offering of burning embers and coca is made before the *awkis*, asking for strength and fertility and for protection for the coming year (fig. 5.12).

The owner of the animals emerges from the house with the newly made llama-hair ropes. In the corral women carry these ropes among the animals while the men play flutes, and all sing and drink. A cloth is spread on the ground and the special ropes, bells, and coca leaves are placed upon it. Members of the family tie or hold the animals by the ears, pulling their heads back, and force them to drink the same maize beer that the Q'ero family has been drinking all day (fig. 5.13). Later, tassels are sewn in the

**Fig. 5.13 Forcing a male
llama to drink maize
beer, Wañuna Pampa.
Photo by Emilio
Rodriguez, 1977.**

animals' ears and the llamas are released.

Then in the house, with continued drinking, chanting, offerings of beer and coca, music and singing, the ritual goes on all night in a stoned and drunken state of hallucination. Gourds full of beer are consumed and the cup is hurled the length of the room. Eventually the men dance like llamas, shake bells, growl like animals, and hit each other with the ropes as if they were being herded. The music, weaving, stories, and food are all integrated into this religious ceremony that mediates between the gods, the animals, and the people.

Steven Webster notes that the Q'ero took pride in drinking very little alcohol, and that their beer is relatively weak. He suggests that some of the drunkenness apparent at festivals is learned or socially expected behavior.

Phalchay

The *Phalchay* festival celebrates the importance of the alpacas and the people address the *awkis* for the health and fertility of the animals. This is the time of year when the alpacas are giving birth and mating. *Phalcha* is also the name of a red flower (gentian) that grows at high altitudes and is in blossom at that time (February and March). The Q'eros gather these beautiful flowers to use in their festival for the alpacas.

Like so many other cultural elements in the Andes, there is a mixture of Spanish and Andean elements, and the sequence of events around *Phalchay* moves from Spanish to Andean and back. It is preceded by the election of new governing officials of Q'ero who are then feasted and go to Paucartambo to register their authority (*Chayampuy*).[17]

At the start of the *Phalchay* festivals that John Cohen observed, some individual Q'ero men perform a *despacho* the night before. In the morning, they bring a rectangle of sod from the pasture and put it on the floor of the house, and they put

little clay statues of the animals on the sod and offer maize beer, flute music, and songs to these representations of the animals. (Afterwards the sod is returned to the pasture.) Then they drive the flocks up to the pasture, throwing flowers at the animals as they go, still singing and playing flutes. Some families carry white flags on poles, which they parade around the perimeters of the fields adjoining their houses. They stop and perform a separate ritual with drinking and songs, and the women all sing simultaneously, but each with their own individual text, addressed to the *apus* and *awkis* (fig. 5.14).

In these songs they recite their concerns and personal histories, always ending with the words, "Scatter the *phalcha* flower, Waman," a reference to the mountain spirits (Wamanripa is the name of a nearby peak). Each person's song is improvised and allows for an individual outpouring of emotion, an opening up and voicing of pent-up feelings. But the repeated ritualized line about scattering the flowers is addressed to Waman, which is the word for a hawk or eagle that represents the *apu*. In this way, they can avoid addressing the god directly. The lineage of the alpacas is referred to as "mother." *Panti* refers to the pink color of the flowers. The *phalcha* flower itself is a representation of the *apu*; it grows on the side of the *apu* at high altitudes. When people hurl the flowers at the alpacas, they are throwing something from the *apu* to the animal. The flower also represents fertility, reproduction, and wealth. Late in the day as the flocks return from the pasture, this ritual is repeated in the corrals. This is the song sung by Monica Apasa, in Wañuna Pampa in 1984:[18]

Fig. 5.14 Musicians at the *Phalchay* ceremony. The man is playing a *pinkulu*. Photo by John Cohen, 1989.

Why should I leave him? [the apu]
Scatter the panti *flower, Waman*
Alpaca dung
My black alpaca [male], my Partridge
[name of the alpaca]
Scatter the panti *flower, Waman*
Who doesn't remember the phalcha *flower?*
It is certain that they want it to be Monday
[the day they throw the flowers]
Seed of the panti *flower, Waman*
Is it going to happen this Monday?
Don't leave me, my mother
[lineage of alpacas]
Scatter the panti *flower, Waman*
Why did my mother abandon me?
She left me crying.
What suffering you leave me, my brother
[alpaca]
You leave me sleeping [as if I were dead,
because I die without you]
Waman, my brother sun [the apu]
Why do you leave me, brother?
The red phalcha *flower that I gather*
Scatter the panti *flower, Waman*
The earth hill that I climb
[to the places where they pasture]
you will make blossom.
Come here my mother [lineage]
where I sleep with my lover.
Scatter the panti *flower, Waman.*
Leave those ancient things
[the old male alpacas, now no longer fertile]
My Waman
Mound of earth that I climb [hill – apu]
For what small thing [why] do you remain
unmarried, Waman?
Can you not forget this small thing?
Once dead we can forget [and rest]
My shawl of panti *flowers, Waman*
The people who visited me have left,
drinking [drinking maize beer in the corral]

Would I not drink for this?
Scatter the panti *flower, Waman*
Leave the spirit [of the alpaca] in my corral
I have left a good ball of [chewed] coca
[representing dung, as an offering]
Scatter the panti *flower, Waman*
My mother [the lineage of alpacas]
is drinking.
People die and leave.
Scatter the panti *flower, Waman.*
When I wanted you, young girl
[referring to female alpaca]
My black [male] alpaca with red feet
Scatter the panti *flower, Waman*
You eat by the side of another
Or with the alpacas of [the apu]
Santo Domingo
Scatter the panti *flower, Waman*
My joyful valley with the snow peaks.
I would like to be in my little village.
Scatter the panti *flower, Waman.*
With the little brother and sister [alpacas]
You drank to the earth [Pachamama]
Scatter the panti *flower, Waman*
My young foreigner [alpacas who have come
from other places]
My young traveller
You gave me flowers, Waman [you have
brought me good fortune]

To us you left
The alpacas of Santo Domingo [apu]
Grey phalcha *flower, Waman*
[Suffering] takes away the happiness of my
valley.
Scatter the panti *flower, Waman*
To the sons of men who are troublesome [to
the alpacas]
People who leave and die
One or two of you [the alpacas] have gone
away [have died].
Why should we leave? [Why do we have to
die?]
Scatter the panti *flower, Waman*
Alpaca who leads the way forward [heading
the alpaca herd]
Phalcha flower that I have to give
With your little sister [alpaca]
Why does he nurture me?
Scatter the panti *flower, Waman.*
Wouldn't you nurture me? [Why do you
no longer give me offspring?]
Together you are sleeping.
Scatter the panti *flower, Waman.*
Hurry, move on,
Don't look at me mother [for you are
sacred]
Scatter the panti *flower, Waman.*
Take one more …

Carnival

Early the next day after the *Phalchay* ceremony, the *regidor* (announcer) of the entire Q'ero community travels from house to house making brief visits. He goes from hamlet to hamlet by horse. Some men are still putting the final touches on their brightly colored, shaggy dance slings. For months the women have been weaving new ponchos and shawls in preparation for this day. The wearing of new textiles marks the symbolic renewal of the community, along with the new leadership, and renewal of the alpaca herd.[19] From all the high hamlets throughout Q'ero, the individual families and groups travel down the mountain to the ceremonial village (Q'ero Llaqta) to celebrate the Carnival dance.

On their arrival, the men gather in a small plaza where the Q'ero authorities blow blasts on conch-shell trumpets.[20] Many of the men arrive already drunk. Some ride horses recklessly in a display of power. Steven Webster reports that many of the senior men then dismount, go into the church to pay their respects to the icons, and then come out and verbally harangue the officials sitting at a table in the plaza. It seemed that these new officials were not supposed to let their status go to their heads.

That night the different families visit from house to house, singing, playing flutes, dancing, and sharing maize beer and coca. The music of Carnival is played on four-hole vertical flutes (*pinkulu*) with rectangular notches for note holes (fig. 5.14). These are not found anywhere else in the Andes. They play a distinctive kind of melody limited to four notes,

which makes it recognizably Q'ero. The subject of the song is determined each year by the newly elected mayor of Q'ero, who draws his inspiration from the landscape as he journeys to Paucartambo to present himself. The subjects include *serena* (waterfall, fountain), *turpa* (a flower), *wallata* (wild geese who mate for life and live in the marshland), *waylla* (where the alpaca graze), *kius* (a mythical bird, partridge), and the *phalcha* flower. All the men play *pinkulus*. The instruments are not tuned to each other; they all play in different keys. Neither do they start or finish the melody at the same time. Although this heterophony sounds like musical cacophony to Western ears, it is the maximum expression of the individual. Yet all are playing the same song. These parties and visits go on until late at night. Sometimes a harmonic choral sound emerges, as a kind of musical agreement is achieved, unified by long drone-like notes. But throughout the whole Carnival, nobody hears the music, for they are all participants in it. It is not music to be listened to.

In the morning, everyone gathers in the plaza for the Carnival dance. They utilize all the ritual elements that have already been performed, but in a more intense form shared by the entire community. Groups of women pass out beer, men deliver the drinks in large wooden cups, the authorities blast away on the trumpets, the women sing, the men sing, play flutes, and stomp and whirl around. The women form a ring on the perimeter while the men mix in the center. The men dance an unusual shaking, stomping dance. Groups of women from each family sing the

Carnival song in unison but without regard for the key or timing of the other family groups.

Everyone is wearing their newly woven clothes, featuring bright colors and pristine clean surfaces (fig. 5.15).[21] Groups of men wearing the shaggy, intensely colored dance slings create a dazzling sight (fig. 2.24). Hats worn by men and women are decorated with long streamers of *serpentine* (long curly confetti-like strips of colored paper) as well as flowers. Ribbons with beads are also worn on the *monteras*. Jackets are decorated with an array of decorative white buttons.

These decorations are gaudy but insufficient to obscure the power of the traditional weavings worn by everyone. Especially in the display of new shawls seen draped over the women's shoulders, hanging straight and uncreased down their backs, the incredibly subtle range of variants on the distinctive Q'ero designs become a virtual gallery of textile accomplishment (fig. 5.15). All the pinks and warm reds reflect the color tones of the latest synthetic dyes. In the newest pieces, the patterns cover nearly the entire fabric – there are no background or leftover spaces. The eye moves skittishly from fabric to fabric: there is no place to rest visually. The mixed sounds of voices, flutes, and trumpets duplicate this seemingly chaotic array of visual patterns. And there is no one to contemplate the heterophony and visual jumble because everyone is a participant. For an outsider, this outpouring and assertion of Q'ero identity is a challenging experience. In the midst of the sensory excesses, one becomes aware of the creative richness of

Fig. 5.15 Women at
Carnival (from Flores
et al. 1995, vol. II,
pp. 242–43). Photo
by Jordi Blassi.

an Andean community expressing its sense of self. Tightly shared limits express a single identity, but also allow for great diversity of individual expression.

Both times John Cohen has been at the Q'ero Carnival, around midday during the dance, a severe rain storm hit from the clouds rising from the jungle, and everyone took cover and dispersed, their spirit and clothes dampened briefly. Later there is a big feast shared by the entire community, and then everyone returns home to the isolated hamlets and their quiet lives up in the pastures. The songs

and flute tunes from the festival go on all year, repeated in the pastures. The new textiles eventually become working clothes in the pastures, their designs still evident but faded.

The musical and ritual events that constitute the entire *Phalchay*–Carnival festival follow a sequence that moves from the individual (the *despacho* the night before), to the family (inside the house), to the extended family (rituals for the alpacas in the corrals), to the community (the Carnival dance). This series of events is repeated yearly, in

ordered progression. It reveals a cultural organization within their society distinct from the social structure that anthropologists study. Instead of family lineage, inheritance, and power, it is based on the structure of ritual and music.

In the community music and in the continuity of woven Q'ero traditional images, there is the sense that this has been repeated every year for hundreds of years, and simultaneously in the details of song and patterning, something is taking place that is new and has never been seen before.

Tinkuy

A few days after the Carnival celebration, young couples from Q'ero have a dance up on the high 4600 m (15,000 ft) pass that marks the border between Q'ero and their neighbors from the village of Jachacalla, who weave in the style of the Ocongate area. They refer to the dance as a *tinkuy*, a meeting of opposites, or the flowing together of different forces.[22] For this occasion the Q'ero abandon their flutes and Q'ero music and dance to battery-powered phonographs with 45 rpm records of commercially recorded Carnival and *huayno* music, the predominant popular form of Andean music. Further, they do not wear their distinctive Q'ero clothes, but instead are dressed in ponchos and shawls that are identical to the clothes of their neighbors, but which they weave themselves. For this meeting with the outside world, the Q'eros hide their identity.

Although they were acting now as part of the larger Andean community, the Q'eros achieved this without being assimilated, and without abandoning their traditional practices of the previous week. By disguising themselves in order to protect their Q'ero identity they reveal a capacity to be devious. This kind of practice connects them with Third World native peoples who have adopted similar behavior as reactions to the dominant cultures that encroach upon them. It is their way of defending themselves.

Likewise when they come to the market at Ocongate, a two-day walk across the mountains, they hide their Q'ero costumes. I asked a Q'ero man why they do not wear their Q'ero clothes in town. He said, "People will laugh at us. They say, 'Q'ero, Q'ero.'"[23] It is a testament to their belief in their own traditions that despite such ridicule the Q'ero persist in weaving and wearing their distinctive textiles.

Notes

1. For more on Q'ero *paqos*, see the article by Washington Rozas in Flores and Núñez del Prado (eds.) 1983. Wilcox 1999 provides a popular account.
2. Wilcox 1999, p. 6.
3. For a summary of Q'ero festivals see Müller and Müller 1984b.
4. Yábar's 1922 article (1986, pp. 191–92) describes Carnival dress for that period.
5. There is now a considerable literature on Qoylluriti: Gow 1974, 1976; Müller 1980; Randall 1982, 1987; Sallnow 1974, 1987; Allen 1988, *etc.*
6. Randall (1982, p. 38; 1987), who has been at Qoylluriti eight times, starting in 1979, and also cites a film made in 1974, has observed changes over time.
7. Webster 1972a, pp. 88, 268–69, describes Qoylluriti briefly, having been to Ancasi and Kamara and observed proceedings in Q'ero Llaqta in 1970. He has supplied additional detail for this account, based on his attending the last two days of the pilgrimage at Qoylluriti (but not the traveling) in 1977. A few details mentioned by Müller 1980, who went to Qoylluriti with the Q'ero in 1980, are also included.
8. Müller 1980, pp. 58, 63 (also Müller and Müller 1984b, p. 173). Although Müller could have seen the stone, he would not have observed the ritual at Kamara in the same year as he went to Qoylluriti.
9. See also the photographs in Müller and Müller 1986, p. 137 and Silverman 1986b, p. 65, fig. 4; 1990, p. 157, fig. 6; 1993, p. 36 top; 1998, p. 158, fig. 7.8.
10. Patricia J. Lyon, personal communication 2001.
11. Cohen 1991, cuts 18–21, 37; Getzels and Gordon 1985. Sallnow (1974, p. 108; 1987, p. 300) gives the melody in musical notation.
12. Silverman 1989, p. 20. Wilcox (1999, p. 73) mentions Qolla dancers in the 1995 pilgrimage.
13. Allen 1983.
14. The Q'ero stone is mentioned by Wilcox 1999, p. 74, but Webster was not told of it. Wilcox also says there are two other sacred places and an *apu*, Qolquepunku, near Qoylluriti at which ceremonies are performed by the Q'eros.
15. Gow 1974, pp. 65–66, 1976, p. 225; Randall 1982, p. 44; Allen 1988, p. 196. Müller and Müller (1984b, pp. 174–75) mention these rituals for the Q'eros, though they are not included in Müller 1980.
16. Sallnow 1974, p. 136; 1987, pp. 220–21.
17. Webster 1972a, p. 189.
18. Translation by Jubernal Díaz, Washington Rozas, and Penelope Harvey. Mannheim 1998 discusses another *Phalcha* song from Q'ero. See also Müller and Müller 1986, p. 228.
19. Webster 1975, p. 147.
20. See Cohen's film (1990), *Carnival in Q'eros*, made at the 1989 festival.
21. For more photographs of *Phalchay* and Carnival in Q'ero, see Flores *et al.* 1995, vol. II, pp. 229–57.
22. This *tinkuy* is shown at the end of Cohen's film (1984).
23. See Cohen 1990.

Bibliography

Albers, Anni
1965
On Weaving. Wesleyan University Press, Middletown, Connecticut.

Allen, Catherine J.
1983
Of Bear-Men and He-Men: Bear Metaphors and Male Self-Perceptions in a Peruvian Community, *Latin American Indian Literatures*, vol. 7, no. 1, pp. 38–51. Department of Hispanic Languages and Literature, University of Pittsburgh.

1988
The Hold Life Has: Coca and Cultural Identity in an Andean Community. Smithsonian Institution Press, Washington, D.C. and London.

Antúnez de Mayolo, Kay K.
1989
Peruvian Natural Dye Plants, *Economic Botany*, vol. 43, no. 2, pp. 181–91. New York Botanical Garden, Bronx.

Arguedas, José María
1967
Mitos quechuas pre-hispanicos, *Amaru. Revista de artes y ciencias*, no. 3, July–September, pp. 14–18. Universidad Nacional de Ingeniería, Lima. Reprinted in Holzmann 1986, pp. 129–32.

Benavente García, Adelma
1995
The Cusco School: Photography in Southern Peru, 1900–1930, *Peruvian Photography: Images from the Southern Andes, 1900–1945*, pp. 8–12. University of Essex, Colchester. Reprinted in *History of Photography*, vol. 24, no. 2, summer 2000, pp. 101–05. Taylor & Francis, London and Philadelphia.

Bird, Junius B.
1960
Suggestions for Recording of Data on Spinning and Weaving and the Collecting of Material, *The Kroeber Anthropological Society Papers*, no. 22, spring, pp. 1–9. Department of Anthropology, University of California, Berkeley. Reprinted by The Textile Museum, Washington, D.C., 1976.

1969
Handspun Yarn Production Rates in the Cuzco Region of Peru, *Textile Museum Journal*, vol. II, no. 3, December 1968, pp. 9–16. Washington, D.C.

Cahlander, Adele, with Elayne Zorn and Ann Pollard Rowe
1980
Sling Braiding of the Andes. Weaver's Journal Monograph IV, Colorado Fiber Center, Boulder.

Cason, Marjorie, and Adele Cahlander
1976
The Art of Bolivian Highland Weaving. Watson-Guptill Publications, New York.

Cohen, John
1957
Q'eros: A Study in Survival, *Natural History*, vol. LXVI, no. 9, November, pp. 482–93. American Museum of Natural History, New York.

1979
Qeros: The Shape of Survival. Film/video. Video distributed by Mystic Fire Video, New York, and University of California Extension, Center for Media and Independent Learning, Berkeley.

1980
Peruvian Weaving: A Continuous Warp for 5000 Years. Film/video. Video distributed by University of California Extension, Center for Media and Independent Learning, Berkeley.

1984
Mountain Music of Peru. Film/video. Video distributed by University of California Extension, Center for Media and Independent Learning, Berkeley.

1987
Among the Qeros: Notes from a Filmmaker, *Folklife Annual 1986*, pp. 22–41. American Folklife Center at the Library of Congress, Washington, D.C.

1990
Carnival in Q'eros. Film/video. Video distributed by the University of California Extension, Center for Media and Independent Learning, Berkeley.

1991
Mountain Music of Peru, vol. I. Folkways CD SF 40020, Smithsonian Institution, Washington, D.C. Reissue with additional material and revised notes. Cuts 12–40 were recorded in Q'ero. Originally released on LP in 1966 (Folkways FE 4539). Notes to the 1966 edition reprinted in Holzmann 1986, pp. 205–20.

1998
Q'ero, *The Garland Encyclopedia of World Music*, ed. Dale Olsen, pp. 225–31. Garland Publishing, New York and London.

MS
An Investigation of Contemporary Weaving of the Peruvian Indians. Master's thesis, Dept. of Design, Yale University, New Haven Connecticut, 1957. Copy deposited in the library of The Textile Museum, Washington, D.C.

Dean, Carolyn
1999
Inka Bodies and the Body of Christ. Duke University Press, Durham and London.

Escobar Moscoso, Mario
1958
Reconocimiento geográfico de Q'ero, *Revista universitaria*, año XLVII, no. 115, pp. 159–88. Universidad Nacional del Cuzco. Reprinted in Flores *et al.*, eds., 1983, pp. 1–13; and Holzmann 1986, pp. 55–97, but without the 20 photos and 2 drawings.

Ferris, H. B.
1916
The Indians of Cuzco and the Apurimac. Memoirs of the American Anthropological Association, vol. III, no. 2, April–June. Lancaster, Pennsylvania.

Flores Ochoa, Jorge A., and Ana María Fries
1989
Puna, qheswa, yunga. *El hombre y su medio in Q'ero.* Colecciones andinas. Banco Central de Reserva del Perú, Fondo Editorial, Lima. Text based on Flores *et al.*, eds., 1983, plus information from Efraín Molleapaza and John Cohen.

Flores Ochoa, Jorge A., and Juan V. Núñez del Prado Bejar with Manuel Castillo Farfan, editors
1983
Q'ero. El último ayllu inka. Homenaje a Oscar Núñez del Prado. Centro de Estudios Andinos, Cuzco. The authors are: Oscar Núñez del Prado Castro, Juan V. Núñez del Prado Bejar, Mario Escobar Moscoso, Steven S. Webster, Gail P. Silverman-Proust, Washington Rozas Alvarez, Efraín Morote Best, and Peter Getzels. Some new and some reprinted material.

Flores Ochoa, Jorge A., Kim MacQuarrie, and Javier Portús (text), Jaume Blassi and Jordi Blassi (photographs)
1995
Gold of the Andes: The Llamas, Alpacas, Vicuñas and Guanacos of South America. 2 vols. Francis O. Patthey and Sons, Barcelona. Available from Amazon.com.

Franquemont, Christine
1986
Chinchero Pallays: An Ethnic Code, *The Junius B. Bird Conference on Andean Textiles*, April 7 and 8, 1984, ed. Ann Pollard Rowe, pp. 331–37. The Textile Museum, Washington, D.C.

Franquemont, Edward M.
1985
Andean Spinning … Slower by the Hour, Faster by the Week, *Spin-Off*, vol. IX, no. 1, spring, pp. 54–55. Interweave Press, Loveland, Colorado.

1986
Cloth Production Rates in Chinchero, Peru, *The Junius B. Bird Conference on Andean Textiles*, April 7 and 8, 1984, ed. Ann Pollard Rowe, pp. 309–29. The Textile Museum, Washington, D.C.

Franquemont, Edward M., and Christine Robinson Franquemont
1988
Learning to Weave in Chinchero, *The Textile Museum Journal*, vol. 26 (1987), pp. 54–78. Washington, D.C.

Franquemont, Edward M., Christine Franquemont, and Billie Jean Isbell
1992
Awaq ñawin. El ojo del tejedor. La práctica de la cultura en el tejido, *Revista andina*, año 10, no. 1, July, issue 19, pp. 47–80. Centro "Bartolomé de Las Casas," Cuzco.

Getzels, Peter, and Harriet Gordon
1985
In the Footsteps of Taytacha. Film/video. Documentary Educational Resources, Watertown, Massachusetts.

Goodell, Grace
1969
A Study of Andean Spinning in the Cuzco Region, *Textile Museum Journal*, vol. II, no. 3, December 1968, pp. 2–8. Washington, D.C.

Gow, David Drummon
1974
Taytacha Qollur Rit'i, *Allpanchis*, vol. VII, November, pp. 49–100. Instituto de Pastoral Andina, Cuzco.

1976
The Gods and Social Change in the High Andes. PhD dissertation, Anthropology, University of Wisconsin, Madison. University Microfilms International, Ann Arbor, Michigan.

Holzmann, Rodolfo
1980
Cuatro ejemplos de música q'ero (Cuzco, Perú), *Latin American Music Review/Revista de música latinoamericana*, vol. 1, no. 1, pp. 74–91. University of Texas Press, Austin.

1986
Q'ero, pueblo y música. Un estudio etnomusicológico basado en 33 piezas del repertorio vocal e instrumental de los Q'eros. Con la inserción de todos los trabajos anteriores publicados sobre Q'ero, 15 fotografías, 3 mapas y un disco de música q'ero. Patronato Popular y Provenir, Pro Música Clásica, Lima. Includes an analog 33⅓ rpm sound disk.

LeCount, Cynthia Gravelle
1990
Andean Folk Knitting: Traditions and Techniques from Peru and Bolivia. Dos Tejedoras Fiber Arts Publications, St. Paul, Minnesota.

Mackey, Carol, Hugo Pereyra, Carlos Radicati, Humberto Rodriguez, Oscar Valverde, editors
1990
Quipu y yupana. Colección de escritos. Consejo Nacional de Ciencia y Tecnología (CONCYTEC), Lima.

Mannheim, Bruce
1998
A Nation Surrounded, *Native Traditions in the Post-Conquest World*, ed. Elizabeth Hill Boone and Tom Cummins, pp. 383–420. Dumbarton Oaks Research Library and Collections, Washington, D.C.

Martinez Escobar, Gabriela, and Elke van der Hoeven
1993
Textiles in the Southern Andes. Taruka Films of Peru. Video distributed by University of California Extension, Center for Media and Independent Learning, Berkeley.

Meisch, Lynn A., editor
1997
Traditional Textiles of the Andes: Life and Cloth in the Highlands: The Jeffrey Appleby Collection of Andean Textiles. Thames & Hudson, New York, and Fine Arts Museums of San Francisco.

Mercado, Edith
1995
La tiklla. Técnica andina en extinción, *Revista del Museo e Instituto de Arqueología, Museo Inka*, no. 25, pp. 181–90. Universidad Nacional de San Antonio Abad del Cuzco.

Morote Best, Efraín
1958
Un nuevo mito de fundación del imperio, *Revista del Instituto Americano de Arte*, año VIII, no. 8, pp. 38–58. Cuzco. Reprinted in Flores *et al.*, eds., 1983, pp. 158–69 and Holzmann 1986, pp. 143–71.

Müller, Thomas
1980
Taytacha Qoyllur Rit'i, *Pastoral andina*, no. 32, pp. 51–66. Instituto de Pastoral Andina, Cuzco.

Müller, Thomas, and Helga Müller
1984a
Mito de Inkarri-Qollari (cuatro narraciones), with an introduction by Juan Ossio Acuña, *Allpanchis*, no. 23, año XIV, vol. XX, pp. 125–43. Instituto de Pastoral Andina, Cuzco.

1984b
Cosmovisión y celebraciones del mundo andino a traves del ejemplo de la comunidad de Q'ero (Paucartambo), *Allpanchis*, no. 23, año XIV, vol. XX, pp. 161–76. Instituto de Pastoral Andina, Cuzco.

Müller, Thomas, and Helga Müller-Herbon
1986
Kinder der Mitte. Die Q'ero Indianer. Lamuv Verlag, Bornheim. Second printing, Göttingen, 1993.

Nectoux, Jean-Michel, editor
1989
Afternoon of a Faun: Mallarmé, Debussy, Nijinsky. The Vendome Press, New York and Paris.

Noble, Carol Rasmussen
1982
Peruvian Slings: Their Uses and Regional Variations, *The Weaver's Journal*, vol. VI, no. 4, issue 24, spring, pp. 53–56. Colorado Fiber Center, Boulder.

Núñez del Prado Castro, Oscar
1950
El kipu moderno, *Tradición. Revista peruana de cultura*, año I, vol. II, nos. 3–6. Cuzco. Reprinted in Mackey *et al.*, eds., 1990, pp. 165–82.

1957
El hombre y la familia. Su matrimonio y organización politico-social en Q'ero. Editorial Garcilaso, Cuzco. Reprinted 1970. Also reprinted in *Revista universitaria*, año XLVII, no. 114, pp. 1–23. Cuzco, 1958; *Allpanchis*, vol. I, pp. 5–27, Instituto de Pastoral Andina, Cuzco, 1969; Flores *et al.*, eds., 1983, pp. 106–30; Holzmann 1986, pp. 25–54, but without the 11 photos.

1968
Una cultura como respuesta de adaptación al medio andino, *Actas y memorias*, 37th Congreso Internacional de Americanistas, Buenos Aires, 1966, vol. IV, pp. 241–60. Reprinted in Flores *et al.*, eds., 1983, pp. 14–29.

1973
Version del mito de Inkarrí en Q'eros, *Ideología mesiánica del mundo andino*, ed. Juan M. Ossio A., pp. 276–80. Edición de Ignacio Prado Pastor, Lima.

1983
El maíz q'ero como solución a algunos problemas de alimentación en la ceja de selva, *Evolución y tecnología de la agricultura andina*, ed. Mario Tapia and Ana María Fríes, pp. 39–44. Cuzco.

Quiggle, Charlotte
2000
Alpaca: An Ancient Luxury, *Interweave Knits*, vol. V, no. 1, fall, pp. 24–26. Interweave Press, Loveland, Colorado.

Paul, Anne
1992
Procedures, Patterns, and Deviations in Paracas Embroidered Textiles, *To Weave for the Sun: Andean Textiles in the Museum of Fine Arts, Boston*, by Rebecca Stone-Miller, pp. 25–33. Museum of Fine Arts, Boston.

Poole, Deborah
1997
Vision, Race, and Modernity: A Visual Economy of the Andean Image World. Princeton University Press, Princeton, New Jersey.

Randall, Robert
1982
Qoyllur Rit'i, an Inca Fiesta of the Pleiades: Reflections on Time and Space in the Andean World, *Boletín del Instituto Francés de Estudios Andinos*, tomo XI, nos. 1–2, pp. 37–81. Lima.

1987
Return of the Pleiades, *Natural History*, vol. 96, no. 6, June, pp. 42–53. Photographs by Norris Ogard. American Museum of Natural History, New York.

Ranney, Edward
2000
New Light on the Cusco School: Juan Manuel Figueroa Aznar and Martín Chambi, *History of Photography*, vol. 24, no. 2, summer, pp. 113–20. Taylor & Francis, London and Philadelphia.

Rowe, Ann Pollard
1975
Weaving Processes in the Cuzco Area of Peru, *Textile Museum Journal*, vol. IV, no. 2, pp. 30–46. Washington, D.C.

1977a
Warp-Patterned Weaves of the Andes. The Textile Museum, Washington, D.C.

1977b
Weaving Styles in the Cuzco Area, *Ethnographic Textiles of the Western Hemisphere*, Irene Emery Roundtable on Museum Textiles, 1976 Proceedings, ed. Irene Emery and Patricia Fiske, pp. 61–84. The Textile Museum, Washington, D.C.

1978
Prácticas textiles en el área del Cusco, *Tecnología andina*, ed. Rogger Ravines, pp. 369–94. Instituto de Estudios Peruanos, Lima. Spanish translation of Rowe 1975.

1997
Inca Weaving and Costume, *The Textile Museum Journal*, vols. 34–35 (1995–96), pp. 4–53. Washington, D.C.

Sallnow, Michael J.
1974
La peregrinación andina, *Allpanchis*, vol. VII, November, pp. 101–42. Instituto de Pastoral Andina, Cuzco.

1987
Pilgrims of the Andes: Regional Cults in Cusco. Smithsonian Institution Press, Washington, D.C., and London.

Seibold, Katharine E.
1992
Textiles and Cosmology in Choquecancha, Cuzco, Peru, *Andean Cosmologies Through Time: Persistence and Emergence*, ed. Robert V.H. Dover, Katharine E. Seibold, and John H. McDowell, pp. 166–201. Indiana University Press, Bloomington and Indianapolis.

Sekino, Yoshiharu
1984
Kero: Harukanaru Inka no Mura/Q'ero: Outlived Inca Village. Asahi Shimbun Company, Tokyo (Japanese text, Japanese and English captions).

Silverman-Proust, Gail P.
1984
Los motivos de los tejidos de Q'ero. La descripción de los tejidos, *Revista del Museo e Instituto de Arqueología*, vol. 23, pp. 281–308. Universidad Nacional de San Antonio de Abad del Cuzco.

1985
El motivo diamante de cuatro partes. Símbolo del tiempo y espacio andinos, *Actas y trabajos, VI Congreso Peruano. Hombre y cultura andina*, ed. Francisco E. Iriarte Brenner, vol. 2, pp. 73–113. Universidad Inca Garcilaso de la Vega, Facultad de Ciencias Sociales, Asociación Peruano Alemana de Arqueología, Instituto Nacional de Cultura, Lima.

1986a
Cuatro motivos inti de Q'ero, *Boletín de Lima*, año 8, no. 43, January, pp. 61–76. Editorial los Pinos, Lima.

1986b
Representación gráfica del mito Inkarri en los tejidos q'ero, *Boletín de Lima*, año 8, no. 48, November, pp. 59–71. Editorial los Pinos, Lima.

1987
The Woven Shadow of Time: Four Inti Motifs from Q'ero, *Revista "Diálogo andino,"* no. 6, pp. 107–26. Departamento de Antropología, Geografía e Historia, Universidad de Tarapacá, Arica, Chile.

1988a
Weaving Technique and the Registration of Knowledge in the Cusco area of Perú, *Journal of Latin American Lore*, vol. 14, no. 2, pp. 207–41. University of California, Los Angeles.

1988b
Significado simbólico de las franjas multicolores tejidas en los wayakos de los Q'ero, *Boletín de Lima*, año 10, no. 57, May, pp. 37–44. Editorial los Pinos, Lima.

1989
Tawa inti qocha, símbolo de la cosmología andina. Concepción q'ero del espacio, *Anthropologica*, año VI (1988), no. 6, pp. 7–42. Departamento de Ciencias Sociales, Pontificia Universidad Católica del Perú, Lima.

1990
Representación gráfica del mito Inkarri en los tejidos q'ero, *Mitos universales, americanos y contemporáneos*, compiled by Moisés Lemlij, vol. III, pp. 147–75. Sociedad Peruana de Psicoanalisis, Lima and Universidad San Antonio Abad del Cuzco.

1991
Iskaymanta/kinsamanta. La tecnica de tejer y el libro de la sabiduria elaborado en el departamento del Cuzco, *Boletín de Lima*, año 13, vol. XIII, no. 74, March, pp. 49–66. Editorial los Pinos, Lima. Spanish version of Silverman-Proust 1988a.

Silverman, Gail P.
1994a
Iconografia textil q'ero vista como texto. Leyendo el rombo dualista *Hatun Inti, Boletin de l'Institut Français d'Etudes Andines*, tomo. 23, no. 1, pp. 171–90. Lima.

1994b
La metáfora del cuerpo humano. Una nueva hipótesis en relación al significado de la iconografia de los textiles de Q'ero, *Anthropologica*, año XII, no. 12, pp. 64–85. Departamento de Ciencias Sociales, Pontificia Universidad Católica del Perú, Lima.

1995a
La importancia de las investigaciones etnográficas de los textiles en la arqueología cusqueña, *Boletín de Lima*, año 17, vol. XVII, no. 99, June–August, pp. 39–48. Editorial los Pinos, Lima.

1995b
Q'ero. Tierras, cultivos y viviendas, *Boletín de la Sociedad Geográfica de Lima*, vol. 108, pp. 105–18.

1998
El tejido andino. Un libro de sabiduria. Second edition. Fondo de Cultura Económica, Lima. First edition published in 1994 by the Banco Central de Reserva del Perú, Lima. (Contains information from earlier articles.)

1999
Iconografia textil de Cusco y su relacion con los tocapu inca/Textile Iconography from Cusco and its Relation to Inca Toqapu, *Tejidos milenarios del Peru/Ancient Peruvian Textiles*, ed. José Antonio de Lavalle and Rosario de Lavalle de Cardenas, pp. 803–36. AFP Integra, Lima.

Silverman, Gail P., and Sergia Chauca
1993
Ch'unchu pallay. Awana Wasi del Cusco, tomo III. Pontificia Universidad Católica del Peru, Lima (English and Spanish).

Soukup, Jaroslav
1971
Vocabulario de los nombres vulgares de la flora peruana. Colegio Salesiano, Lima.

Switzer, Chris
1994
Spinning Llama and Alpaca. Switzer Land Enterprises, Estes Park, Colorado.

Webster, Steven
1972a
The Social Organization of a Native Andean Community. PhD dissertation, Dept. of Anthropology, University of Washington, Seattle. University Microfilms International, Ann Arbor, Michigan.

1972b
An Indigenous Quechua Community in Exploitation of Multiple Ecological Zones, *Actas y memorias del XXXIX Congreso Internacional de Americanistas,* Lima, 1970, vol. 3, pp. 174–83 and *Revista del Museo Nacional,* 1971, vol. 37, pp. 174–83, Lima. Spanish translation published in Flores *et al.,* eds. 1983, pp. 30–47.

1973
Native Pastoralism in the South Central Andes, *Ethnology,* vol. 12, no. 2, April, pp. 115–33. University of Pittsburgh. Spanish translation published in Flores *et al.* eds., 1983, pp. 48–81 (except first paragraph).

1975
Factores de posición social en una comunidad nativa quechua, *Estudios andinos,* año 4, vol. IV, no. 2 (1974–76), pp. 131–59. Issue 11: Conflicto e integración en los Andes, ed. Ralph Bolton and Sylvia Forman. Centro de Investigación, Universidad del Pacífico, Lima and Center for Latin American Studies, University Center for International Studies, University of Pittsburgh.

1976
Parentesco y afinidad en una comunidad nativa quechua, *Tinkuy,* no. 2, pp. 52–73. Reprinted in *Parentesco y matrimonio en los Andes,* ed. Ralph Bolton and Enrique Mayer. Fondo Editorial, Pontificia Universidad Católica, Lima, 1980. Spanish translation of Webster 1977.

1977
Kinship and Affinity in a Native Quechua Community, *Andean Kinship and Marriage,* ed. Ralph Bolton and Enrique Mayer, pp. 28–42. Special publication no. 7, American Anthropological Association, Washington, D.C. English original of Webster 1976.

1980
Ethnicity in the Southern Peruvian Highlands, *Environment, Society, and Rural Change in Latin America: The Past, Present, and Future in the Countryside,* ed. David A. Preston, pp. 135–54. John Wiley & Sons, Chichester and New York.

1981
Interpretation of an Andean Social and Economic Formation, *Man,* n.s., vol. 16, no. 4, December, pp. 616–33. Royal Anthropological Institute, London.

Wilcox, Joan Parisi
1999
Keepers of the Ancient Knowledge: The Mystical World of the Q'ero Indians of Peru. Element, Boston.

Wilson, David J.
1999
The Q'eros Quechua, *Indigenous South Americans of the Past and Present: An Ecological Perspective,* pp. 304–17. Westview Press, Boulder, Colorado (based on Webster 1972a).

Wilson, Lee Anne
1991
Nature Versus Culture: The Image of the Uncivilized Wild-Man in Textiles from the Department of Cuzco, Peru, *Textile Traditions of Mesoamerica and the Andes: An Anthology,* ed. Margot Blum Schevill, Janet Catherine Berlo, and Edward B. Dwyer, pp. 205–30. Garland Publishing, New York and London.

Yábar Palacio, Luis
1922
El ayllu de Qqueros–Paucartambo, *Revista universitaria,* año XI, no. 38, September, pp. 2–26. Universidad del Cuzco. Reprinted in Holzmann 1986, pp. 173–96.

1923
Los malditos. El pueblo de los viudos y los "Wachipayres" (de "El ayllu de Qqueros"), *Más allá. Revista mensual literario-científica,* año II, no. 6, pp. 47–50. Cuzco.

Zorn, Elayne
1979
Warping and Weaving on a Four-Stake Ground Loom in the Lake Titicaca Basin Community of Taquile, Peru, *Looms and Their Products,* Irene Emery Roundtable on Museum Textiles, 1977 Proceedings, ed. Irene Emery and Patricia Fiske, pp. 212–27. The Textile Museum, Washington, D.C.

1981
Sling Braiding in the Macusani Area of Peru, *Textile Museum Journal,* vols. 19–20 (1980–81), pp. 41–54. Washington, D.C.

1986
Textiles in Herders' Ritual Bundles of Macusani, Peru, *The Junius B. Bird Conference on Andean Textiles,* April 7 and 8, 1984, ed. Ann Pollard Rowe, pp. 289–307. The Textile Museum, Washington, D.C.

1987
Análisis de los tejidos en los atados rituales de los pastores, *Revista andina,* año 5, no. 2, issue 10, pp. 489–526. Centro "Bartolomé de Las Casas," Cuzco. Spanish version of Zorn 1986.

Zorn, Elayne, and Juan Cutipa Colque
1985
A Closer Look at Alpacas and How they Differ from their Llama Cousins, *Spin-Off,* vol. IX, no. 2, summer, pp. 21–23. Interweave Press, Loveland, Colorado.

Index